The Signs of Hypocrites

For other titles in this series
Please visit www.ibtbooks.com

THE SIGNS OF HYPOCRITES

'A'ID AL-QARNI

IBT

Islamic Book Trust
Kuala Lumpur

Published by
Islamic Book Trust
607 Mutiara Majestic
Jalan Othman
46000 Petaling Jaya
Selangor, Malaysia
www.ibtbooks.com

Islamic Book Trust is affiliated with The Other Press.

Perpustakaan Negara Malaysia Cataloguing-in-Publication Data

Al-Qarni, 'Aidh Abdullah , Dr.
The Signs of Hypocrites / Dr. A'id al-Qarni.
Includes index
ISBN 978-967-0526-28-7
1. Hypocrisy--Religious aspects--Islam.
2. Islamic ethics. 3. Muslims--Conduct of life.
I. Title.
297.5677

Printed by
SS Graphic Printers (M) Sdn. Bhd.
Lot 7 & 8, Jalan TIB 3
Taman Industri Bolton
68100 Batu Caves, Selangor

Contents

CHAPTER 1

Introduction

Surely praise belongs to Allah. We praise Him and seek His help. And we seek refuge in Him from the evil of ourselves and our misdeeds. He whom Allah guides, none can mislead, but He whom He lets go astray, none can guide. And I bear testimony that there is no God but Allah, who is one and has no partner. And I bear witness that Muḥammad (ṣ) is His slave and messenger.

> O you who believe, fear Allah as He should be feared, and die not except as Muslims. (Qur'an 3:102)
>
> O mankind, fear your Lord, Who created you from a single person, and from him He created his mate, and from the twain He spread abroad many men and women. So fear Allah, by Whom you demand (your rights) of one another, and fear (breaking)

> kinship of wombs. Surely Allah is ever watchful over you. (Qur'an 4:1)
>
> O you who believe, fear Allah and speak words straight to the point. He will set right your deeds for you and will forgive your sins. And whosoever obeys Allah and His Messenger, he indeed has gained a mighty triumph. (Qur'an 33:70-71)

The best of words is the Book of Allah and the best of paths is the path of Muḥammad (ṣ). And the worst of affairs are innovations in religion, and every innovation is a straying from the path, and every straying leads to Hell.

When Allah sent His Prophet (ṣ) and he announced his mission, some people rejected him and some believed. Of the latter, some merely put on a garb of faith without really believing, so that they caused mischief. They are called hypocrites. A hypocrite is two-faced and is the worst of mankind. The Prophet (ṣ) said about them,

> "Surely, the worst of men are the two-faced, who come to these with a face and to those with another face."[1]

---

1. *Al-Bukhari*, # 6058.

The hypocrite will incline towards that which seems profitable and is the most dangerous of men. The history of the Muslims bears witness that they have always suffered at the hands of the hypocrites, and it is the same story today. If a ruler is a hypocrite, then Muslims suffer a setback and decline. The Prophet (ṣ) often warned Muslims of hypocrites. He said,

> "What I fear most for my *ummah* is every eloquent-tongued hypocrite."[2]

This is why the Companions and their successors in every generation were ever wary of hypocrisy. And every Muslim must always be cautious and fearful of it and he must keep away from everything that is liable to help it grow. Once it encroaches into his heart, it keeps spreading and growing and might even cause a dent in his faith, leading him to the deepest pit of Hell. Alternatively, it might involve him in major sins and he might not repent, as a result of which he would go to Hell, or the reward for his deeds might be reduced because of his hypocrisy.

Today, the malady of hypocrisy has made inroads

---

2. *Al-Jami' al-Saghir*, # 239.

among Muslims. This book is meant to induce them to shun hypocritical deeds and to help them recognize hypocrites. I hope my effort will benefit me and other Muslims. I have not targeted any individual, organisation or party, but my presentation is of a general nature. Those possessing these signs will be recognized.

CHAPTER 2

Definition of Hypocrisy

The word for hypocrisy in Arabic (*nifāq*) comes from the word for a wild rat's underground tunnel (*nafiqah*), one end of which is hidden and the other visible. The hypocrite is called so because he hides disbelief while declaring belief. Al-Hasan defined hypocrisy thus:

> It is said that hypocrisy is the difference between secret and apparent, between word and deed, between entry and exit. And it is said that the foundation on which hypocrisy is built is falsehood.[3]

3. Al-Faryabi, *Sifah al-Nifaq*, # 50.

Kinds of Hypocrisy

There are two kinds of hypocrisy: that which concerns belief, and that which concerns practice.

Hypocrisy in belief is to prefer the convictions of the infidels, to associate partners with Allah, to despise Allah's Messenger (ṣ), to conceal belief while pretending to believe, to practice contrary to the declaration of faith, to prefer another to Allah for judgment and to prefer the command of anyone other than the Prophet (ṣ). Such people were undoubtedly infidels. They have concealed disbelief to promote their blameworthy aims. Instead of defending the religion, they try to smother the faith of the Muslims and cast doubt in their minds about the Prophet (ṣ). Sometimes they fight against the Muslims out of hatred and jealousy, but when their motives demand it, they do not hesitate to display immense love for the Muslims.

Hypocrisy in practice does not expel a person from Islam but makes him resemble a hypocrite. He has one of the signs of hypocrisy, like falsehood, betrayal of trust, promise-breaking, abusiveness, revilement and so on. Scholars are in agreement that such a person does not come out of the fold of Islam but is definitely a great sinner and there always is the likelihood of his becoming a hypocrite in belief.

In this regard, Hafiz ʻAbd al-Salam Ibn Muḥammad says: "If a believer happens to commit these sins once in a while, then he does not classify as a hypocrite, because believers are also prone to commit sins. But if the sin is committed habitually, then the person is a hypocrite. If all these signs are found in someone, then it is impossible that he believes in Allah and His Messenger (ṣ) sincerely. Thus, if he is a confirmed liar, never fulfils his promises and is given to betray, then he is a hypocrite not only in practice but also in belief, because faith is included in speech and in practice. Falsehood is alien to believers. Allah says:

> It is those who believe not in the signs of Allah that forge falsehood; it is they who lie. (Qur'an 16:105)

The Prophet (ṣ) said, "Keep away from falsehood, for falsehood leads to immorality, and immorality leads to Hell."[4]

---

4. *Al-Bukhari*, # 6094.

The root causes of Hypocrisy

History reveals that one of the following three things causes hypocrisy to grow:

1. *Greed*: When Islam gains ground and spreads and Muslims have the power to decide, some sick souls surface and infiltrate high ranks to further their nefarious designs.

2. *Jealousy*: Some of the people who infiltrate Muslim ranks harbour malice towards Islam and the Muslims whom they try to harm Islam through deception. They pretend to embrace Islam to save their skin but inwardly they disbelieve and are very jealous and wicked. Outwardly, they express love for Muslims and show that they have a missionary zeal.

3. *Trial*: When believers face trials through persecution at the hands of tyrants and are consigned to death because of their beliefs, only the sincere persevere. Hypocrites, on the other hand, seek refuge with disbelievers.

Signs of Hypocrisy

The Prophet (ṣ) said that a hypocrite has four signs. These four signs are not those of hypocrisy in belief, but those of hypocrisy in practice, so whoever has them is a sinner but is not cast out of Islam. However, one who continues to behave in this way will end up a hypocrite in belief. The Prophet (ṣ) made mention of these because they are important and are generally found in hypocrites, but there are many other signs.

In one tradition, the Prophet (ṣ) named only three signs: falsehood, betrayal and cheating. Actually, dishonesty is of three kinds: in speech, in deed and in intention. They are, respectively, falsehood, betrayal of trust and promise-breaking. When there is no trust, faith vanishes. I will try to elaborate on all the signs and deeds of hypocrites in the light of the Qur'an, the tradition and the sayings of the Companions and their successors.

Chapter 3

The Hypocrite's Character

As for him who is given his record in his right hand, he will say,

> "Take! Read my book! Surely I knew that I would have to meet my reckoning." (Qur'an 69:19-20)

Al-Hasan said, "The believer has a good opinion of his Lord, so he does good deeds. But the hypocrite has a bad opinion of his Lord, so he does bad deeds."[5]

Bilal Ibn Sa'd said, "The hypocrite speaks that which is regarded as piety but does what is evil."[6]

Al-Hasan said, "People are of three kinds: believers, hypocrites and disbelievers. The believer

---

5 Al-Faryabi, *Sifah al-Nifaq*, # 96.

6 al-Bayhaqi, *Su'ab al-Iman*, # 6873.

does deeds in obedience to Allah. As for the disbeliever, Allah has disgraced him, as you can see. As for the hypocrite, he is here, on mountains, in homes and on streets. We seek refuge in Allah! By Allah, they did not recognize their Lord, but remember to deny their Lord through their deeds, the wicked deeds. Ignorance and darkness are seen, while knowledge has diminished and the *Sunnah* is forsaken. To Allah we belong and to Him is our return ... They are not Jews or Christians or Magians that they should be excused."

Surely the believer does not take his religion from the people, but it comes to him from Allah and he takes it. The hypocrite gives his tongue to the people but denies to Allah his heart and his deeds. So two new kinds of young people are born in Islam. One has a bad idea and imagines that paradise is for only those who have the same opinions as he. He has unleashed his sword, shed the blood of Muslims and regarded as lawful their sacred belongings. The other is the cruel one who gets his wish and is not stopped by anyone. The world is what he worships and he goes into a rage because of it, even killing and fighting for it.

> Have you considered him who takes his caprice to be his god? (Qur'an 45:23)

Regarding this verse, al-Hasan said, "He is the hypocrite who does whatever he likes." Qatadah said, "He is one who gets done whatever he wants to do."

Hypocrites are the Devil's army, Allah says:

> Satan has gained mastery over them, so he has made them forget Allah's remembrance. Those are Satan's party. Behold, surely Satan's party are the losers! (Qur'an 58:19)

The hypocrites will follow the Dajjal. When he comes before the Last Day, the believers will be safe from his mischief. The hypocrites in Makkah and Madinah, both men and women, will go and join the Dajjal because of earthquakes in these cities. The Prophet (ṣ) said, "The Dajjal will travel all over the earth but not to Makkah and Madinah. When he goes towards Madinah, he will find rows of angels at every road leading to it. Then he will come to a highland of Jarf (a road towards Sham about a mile away). He will encamp there and pitch tents. Then Madinah will shake thrice with earthquakes and the hypocrites, both men and women, will go to the Dajjal."

To not drink the water of Zamzam to satiation

A believer uses Allah's blessings and takes advantage of the lawful, blessed things, as the Prophet's Companions did so.

The water of Zamzam is blessed. Every Muslim drinks it till he is satiated. He never seems to have had enough. But this is not the case with hypocrites.

Ibn Abi Mulaykah said that he was with Ibn 'Abbas when a man came and sat down by his side. 'Ibn 'Abbas asked him, "Where have you come from?" He said, "I have drunk from Zamzam." He asked, "Did you drink it as it deserves to be drunk?" He asked, "How does it deserve to be drunk, O Ibn 'Abbas?" He said, "Face the *qiblah*, say the name of Allah and drink three times, taking a breath between each. When you have finished, praise Allah. You must drink till you are satiated, for I heard Allah's Messenger say, 'The sign that distinguishes us from hypocrites is that they do not drink from the Zamzam to satiation.'"[7]

---

7 *Sifah al-Nifaq*, # 65.

CHAPTER 4
Falsehood

Lying is the root of all evil. It leads to Hell, brings disgrace, belies testimony and is the base of hypocrisy and disbelief. The Prophet (ṣ) said,

> "You must be truthful, for truth guides to piety, and piety leads to paradise. If a man does not cease to speak the truth and is motivated by truth, he is recorded with Allah as a truthful person. And avoid falsehood, for falsehood leads to immodesty, and immodesty leads to Hell. A person does not cease to speak lies and is motivated by it without being recorded with Allah as a liar."[8]

He also said, "Whoever has four particular signs is a pure hypocrite, and whoever has one of them has

8. *Al-Bukhari*, # 6094.

one sign of hypocrisy till he gives it up: when he is trusted, he betrays the trust; when he speaks, he lies; when he promises, he goes back on his word; and when he disputes, he resorts to abuse."[9]

He may pray regularly, fast non-stop and call himself a Muslim, but if he has these signs, then he is a hypocrite.

According to a tradition narrated by Abu Hurayrah, when the Prophet (ṣ) mentioned the three signs, someone asked, "O Messenger, even if only one remains?" He said, "It does not cease to be in his heart as long as there remains something of it in him."[10]

Allah describes the behaviour of hypocrites thus:

> Of mankind there are some who say, "We believe in Allah and the Last Day" when (in fact) they are not believers. They seek to deceive Allah and those who believe; they do not deceive anyone but themselves but do not realize it. In their hearts is a disease, and Allah has increased their disease. For them is a painful chastisement because they have been lying. (Qur'an 2:8-10)

---

9. *Muslim*, # 59-107.

10. Al-Asbahani, *Sifah al-Nifaq*, # 43.

The hypocrites lie with their tongues but Allah discloses what their hearts hold. Lying is a malady that becomes worse if it is not treated. Though telling the truth may cause trials and tribulations, the ultimate result of doing so is always good. Nowadays, some people maintain that to speak lies is rewarded. But there is no doubt that doing so is sinful and hypocritical, as Allah says:

> And Allah bears witness that the hypocrites are surely liars. (Qur'an 63:1)

A false joke, jest or story is also falls into the same category. The Prophet (ṣ) said, "Woe to someone who lies, who lies when he speaks so that people may laugh. Woe to him. Woe to him."[11]

However, the Prophet (ṣ) did not regard three people as liars:

- a person lying to reconcile Muslims,
- a person lying in war and
- spouses lying to each other.[12]

---

11. *Abu Dawud*, # 4990.

12. *Abu Dawud*, # 4921.

A person may reconcile two differing parties by telling one that the other speaks highly of him and saying similar things to the other. In war, one may issue encouraging statements, such as "So many disbelievers have been killed" and "Reinforcements are on the way." A husband and wife may lie to one another to increase their mutual love.

Any lie apart from these is hypocrisy, whether light-hearted or serious, out of necessity or to fool others, to instigate rulers against someone, to alter a religious ruling, to forge a tradition or to spread false news about a war fought elsewhere. The tradition speaks of "lying in war" only in the very country where it is fought, in order to encourage the fighters and boost their morale or to demoralize the enemy.

The root cause of hypocrisy is falsehood. The other sign of hypocrisy also arise because of falsehood. Hence, we must try to avoid it so that there is no share of hypocrisy in our record of deeds.

False oaths to promote sales or to protect oneself

Hypocrites are quick to take false oaths in order to protect themselves.

> They have taken their oaths as a shield, so they bar (others) from the way of Allah. For them will be a humiliating chastisement. (Qur'an 58:16)

> They have taken their oaths as a shield so that they may bar (others) from the way of Allah. Surely, vile is that what they have been doing. (Qur'an 63:2)

Zayd Ibn Arqam said, "I was with my uncle when I heard 'Abdullah Ibn Ubayy Ibn Salul say (to his henchmen) that they should not spend on those people who were with the Prophet (ṣ) unless they leave him. He also said, 'When we reach Madinah, we will drive away the disgraced people (referring to Muḥammad (ṣ) and his Companions) from Madinah.' I told my uncle of this and he informed the Prophet (ṣ) about it. He summoned 'Abdullah Ibn Ubayy Ibn Salul and his henchmen, but they affirmed on oath that they had said nothing of the sort. So the Prophet (ṣ) accepted his word but rejected mine. This caused me untold grief and I retired to my home. Soon after, Allah revealed the sūrah (al-Munāfiqūn from إِذَا جَاءَكَ الْمُنَافِقُونَ to وَلَكِنَّ الْمُنَافِقِينَ لَا يَعْلَمُونَ. The Prophet (ṣ) sent for me and recited this sūrah to me. Then he said, 'Allah has proved you true.'"[13]

Taking a false oath is a sign of hypocrisy and a major sin. The Prophet (ṣ) said, "The major sins are associating partners with Allah, killing anyone and taking a false oath."[14]

If anyone lies in order to promote sales, then he too falls under the purview of this tradition. The Prophet (ṣ) said,

> "There are three whom Allah will not speak to or look at on the Day of Resurrection: a man who falsely swears that he has been offered for his goods so much more than what he is given, a man who takes a false oath after the *'asr* prayer in order that he might flee with a Muslim's property at that moment ...[15]

False testimony

A false testimony is both a major sin and hypocrisy because it is falsehood. The Prophet (ṣ) said,

---

13. *Al-Bukhari*, # 4900.

14. *Al-Bukhari*, # 6675.

15. *Al-Bukhari*, # 2369.

> "The gravest of major sins is ascribing partners to Allah, disobeying parents, slaying someone and false testimony, false testimony, false testimony!"

False excuse

The hypocrites also use false pretexts. Allah says:

> And among them is he who says, "Give me leave and do not tempt me." Behold, they have (already) fallen into temptation. Surely Hell encompasses the disbelievers. (Qur'an 9:49)

When the Prophet (ṣ) was preparing for the Battle of Tabu, he said to the chief of Banu Salamah, Jadd Ibn Qays, "Are you ready to engage Banu al-Asfar?" He said, "Will you permit me not to participate in *jihad*? Do not involve me in a trial. By Allah, my people know that no one loves women as I do, and I fear I might not withhold myself on seeing the women of Banu al-Asfar." The Prophet (ṣ) turned away from him and said, "I give you permission." Afterwards, this verse was revealed concerning this man[16].

Any word or deed that has something of a lie in it is a major sin. This is why Allah says that a painful

16. *Tafsir Ibn Kathir*, al-Tawbah: 49.

punishment awaits the hypocrites, those who sell by telling lies and other liars. Allah says:

> And for them is a painful chastisement because they have been lying. (Qur'an 9:10)

Chapter 5

Abusing Others

Allah's Messenger (ṣ) said, "A believer does not taunt, does not revile, is not immoral and is not shameless."[17]

The Prophet (ṣ) also said that if anyone possesses four things, then he is a hypocrite, and one of these is that he abuses when he quarrels.

While it is allowed to avenge an abuse, it is not allowed to lie. The Prophet (ṣ) said, "When two men revile one another, whatever they say is against the first one as long as the one wronged does not transgress (in seeking revenge)."[18]

If the one wronged lies against the initiator, then

17. *Al-Tirmidhi*, # 1977.

18. *Muslim*, # 68-2587.

both are hypocritical. The Prophet (ṣ) said, "Two people who revile one another are both devilish, abusers and liars."[19]

But if one of them endures patiently, then it is good for him. Allah says:

> Whosoever defends himself after he has been wronged—against such there is no cause of blame. (Qur'an 42:41)
>
> Indeed if any shows patience and forgives, that would only be an exercise of courageous will and resolution in the conduct of affairs. (Qur'an 42:43)

---

19. *Al-Targhib wa al-Tarhib*, # 4207.

CHAPTER 6

Retracting a Covenant

Allah says about promises:

> Fulfil (your) covenant; surely of the covenant it will be asked. (Qur'an 17:34)

This promise will be made good and the believers will demand it in the same way as a creditor demands his money. The believers are those who fulfil their promises. Allah says:

> Those who faithfully observe their trusts and their covenants (Qur'an 23:8)

But the hypocrites do not fulfil their promises.

> Certainly they had made a covenant with Allah a foretime (that) they would not turn (their) backs. A covenant with Allah will be questioned of. (Qur'an 33:15)

The hypocrites promised to Allah and His Messenger (ṣ) that they would not turn their backs during the war, but they failed to keep their promise.

One of them had promised to give some charity if Allah gave him wealth, but he went back on his promise. The same kind of people exist today, people who spend lavishly on entertainment but only make vain promises to give charity if Allah grants them wealth. Allah says:

> Of them are some who have made a covenant with Allah (saying), "If He gives us out of His bounty, we will certainly give alms and be of the righteous." Yet, when He gave them of His bounty, they became niggardly of it and turned away while they were averse. Hence, He put hypocrisy into their hearts, until the day they meet Him, because they went back on that (word) which they had promised with Allah, and because they used to lie. (Qur'an 9:75-77)

Going back on one's word is a sign of hypocrisy. The Prophet (ṣ) said, as we have seen, that a hypocrite has three signs: he lies when he speaks, he betrays when he promises, and if he is trusted, he proves treacherous.

The Prophet (ṣ) also said, "He who is not faithful

to his trust has no faith, and he who is not true to his promise, has no religion."

This tradition speaks of all kinds of promises a man makes, including one to meet someone somewhere. However, if a person is unable to fulfil his promise in spite of his best efforts, then he is not liable to punishment, as Allah says:

> Allah does not charge a soul save to its capacity (Qur'an 2:286)

CHAPTER 7

To Betray a Trust

To be faithful to one's trust is an attribute of a Muslim. Even before he was commissioned, the Prophet (ṣ) was known as "*al-Amin*" (the Trustworthy) and "*al-Sadiq*" (the Truthful). Allah commands the believers to be faithful to their trusts.

> Surely Allah commands you to restore trusts to their owners. (Qur'an 4:58)

Allah often mentions in the Qur'an that the believer is faithful to his trusts. Describing the successful inheritors of paradise, he says:

> And those who preserve their trusts and their covenant. (Qur'an 70:32)

In contrast, to be unfaithful to trusts is a major sign of hypocrisy, as the Prophet (ṣ) said, "The signs of a hypocrite are three: when he speaks, he lies; when he promises, he goes against it; and when he is entrusted, he betrays. [20]

He also said that a person who betrays his trust has no faith and a person who breaks his promise has no religion.[21]

The meaning of *trust* is very broad. It is not merely to keep some material in trust. The following form part of trusts:

Entrusting money or property

This is what the verse covers:

> Of the people of the Book is he who, if you trust him with a heap of wealth, will restore it to you. And of them is he who, if you trust him with a single dinar, would not restore it to you, unless you are ever present there to demand it. That is because they say, "There is no blame on us in the matter of the illiterates (gentiles)." And they forge a lie against Allah while they know it. (Qur'an 3:75)

This verse speaks of wealth as a trust, just as it is understood in common parlance.

---

20 *Al-Bukhari*, # 73.

21 *Ahmad*, # 3/154.

Religion as a trust

Allah has declared that the *Shari'ah* is a trust with us; we must preserve it and not be treacherous, otherwise we would be not true Muslims, but like polytheists or hypocrites. Allah says:

> Surely we offered the trust to the heavens and the earth and the mountains, but they refused to undertake it and were afraid of it, and man undertook it. Surely, he is very unjust, foolish. (Qur'an 33:72)

Here *trust* includes the commands of *Shari'ah*, the obligatory duties, which one is rewarded for doing and liable to punishment for not doing.

> That Allah may chastise the hypocritical men and hypocritical women and the men and women who associate partners with Him, and that Allah may relent towards the believing men and the believing women. Allah is ever forgiving, merciful. (Qur'an 33:73)

Secret or conversation as trust

If a person confides in another, then that is a trust with him and he is not allowed to disclose it to anyone else. When the Prophet (ṣ) sent Lubabah Ibn 'Abd al-

Mundhir to Banu Qurayzah to command them to come down from their forts, they sought his advice and he pointed to his throat, indicating that they would be executed. So Allah revealed:

> O you who believe, betray not Allah and the Messenger, nor betray your trusts knowingly. (Qur'an 8:27)

That their necks would be severed was a trust with him, but he failed to preserve it. When this verse was revealed, he bound himself to a pillar in the Masjid al-Nabawi, vowing not to eat anything or release himself till Allah accepted his repentance. After nine days, he became unconscious and Allah accepted his repentance.[22]

If a person looks here and there before he speaks to another then his words are a trust with him. The Prophet (ṣ) said, "When a person speaks and turns (here and there), then it is a trust."[23]

In the same way, a meeting or a consultation is a trust when permission is not granted to make the proceedings public. Of course, if a conspiracy is

---

22 *Tafsir Ibn Kathir*, Sūrah al-Anfal: 27.

23 *Abu Dawud*, # 4868.

hatched, say, to kill someone, then such a meeting is not a trust. The Prophet (ṣ) said, "Meetings are trusts unless they are to shed blood, to commit indecency or to misappropriate someone's property."[24]

In fact it is obligatory to disclose the proceedings of meetings where evil things are decided to be done so that people do not suffer unnecessarily. Also, it is not allowed for anyone to compel a member of a meeting to disclose its proceedings.

The private life of a couple is also a trust. The Prophet (ṣ) said, "One of the greatest trusts to Allah on the Day of Resurrection will be a man who had intercourse with his wife and she with him, then he broadcast her secret." [25]

Responsibilities and offices as trust

Upon the conquest of Makkah, the Prophet (ṣ) asked for the key to the Ka'bah and opened its door. As he was coming out, this verse was revealed:

> Surely Allah commands you to restore the trusts to their owners. (Qur'an 4:58)

---

24 *Abu Dawud*, # 4869.

25 *Muslim*, # 124-1438.

'Abbas had suggested that he should be entrusted with the key, too, in addition to the office of providing water, which he already held. But the Prophet (ṣ) restored the key to 'Uthman Ibn Talhah.[26]

Responsibilities should be given to those entitled to them. Before entrusting anyone with a responsibility or an office, he must be examined to see whether he is worthy of it. If the person hands it over without examining him, then he himself betrays his trust. And one who is given a responsibility must do his best to discharge it honestly, otherwise he is treacherous. Thus, a leader should be honest and sincere in his leadership, as should a teacher in his teaching and a treasurer in his handling of cash, otherwise they commit a breach of trust.

When Abu Dharr asked to be appointed to a position of authority, the Prophet (ṣ) told him "O Abu Dharr, you are weak, and this is a trust. On the Day of Resurrection, it will be a source of humiliation and regret except for the one who takes it and fulfils all obligations and does all duties required."[27]

---

26 *Tafsir Ibn Kathir*, 4:58.

27 *Muslim*, #16-1825.

CHAPTER 8
To Deceive

No religion approves of deception. Islam retains every good thing and abolishes everything that is bad. The Prophet (ṣ) laid down a common principle when he said, "He who deceives does not belong to us."[28]

Whenever he sent an army, he instructed the commander to refrain from deceiving anyone. He would instruct him particularly to fear Allah and to be a well-wisher of the Muslims accompanying him. He would say, "Fight in the name of Allah, for His cause. Fight him who rejects Allah. And do not betray, do not deceive, do not mutilate and do not kill children."[29]

---

28 *Muslim*, # 101-164.

29 *Muslim*, # 3-1731.

He gave the instruction not to deceive any advancing army, small unit or caravan. If anyone deceives after concluding a covenant, whether with Muslims, disbelievers, leaders or his subordinates, then he has a major sign of hypocrisy. The Prophet (ṣ) said, "If anyone possesses four traits then he is a hypocrite in the real sense. And he who possesses one of them has one trait of hypocrisy till he abandons it. They are: when he is entrusted, he betrays; when he speaks, he lies; when he promises, he breaches; and when he quarrels, he abuses."[30]

The Prophet (ṣ) said, "On the day of resurrection, every deceiver will have a banner on his back whereby he would be recognized. It will be said that he is the deceiver of so-and-so."[31]

To be Careful of Appearances but to Neglect the hidden

A Muslim is careful to set right both the apparent as well as the hidden aspects of his being. The apparent includes cleanliness and purity and a pleasing

30 *Al-Bukhari*, # 34.

31 *Al-Bukhari*, # 3188.

appearance. Allah loves cleanliness, as the Prophet (ṣ) said, "Surely Allah is beautiful and likes beauty. He loves that the signs of His blessings be seen on His slave, and He dislikes a wretched appearance and pretending to be miserable."[32]

The Prophet (ṣ) also said, "Allah does not look at your faces or your wealth, but He looks at your hearts and your deeds."[33]

While a Muslim performs righteous deeds and develops fear of Allah in His heart, a hypocrite is content with the apparent and gives no thought to his hidden side. His deeds, too, if he has any good deeds at all, he does only to be seen. Allah says:

> And when you see them, their figures please you, and if they speak, you listen to their speech, (yet) they are like propped-up beams of timber. They think every shout (they hear) to be against them. They are the enemy, so beware of them. May Allah destroy them! How they are perverted! (Qur'an 63:4)

Regarding this verse, Zayd Ibn Arqam said that

---

32 *Al-Jami' al-Saghir*, # 1742.

33 *Muslim*, # 34-2564.

the hypocrites were men of apparent beauty.

A believer is worries about the hereafter and spends for Allah's cause. On the other hand, a hypocrite has no worries about the hereafter and does not spend anything for Allah's cause. He takes great care of his outer appearance.

Chapter 9

Neglecting Prayers

After saying the *shahadah*, the obligatory prayers are the base of Islam. Whoever does not observe them intentionally commits a major sin.

The Prophet (ṣ) said, "I have been commanded to fight against the people till they testify that there is no God but Allah and I am Allah's Messenger, they establish the obligatory prayers and pay *zakah*. When they do that, they have protection from me with regard to their blood and their wealth."[34]

He also said, "Between a man and polytheism and disbelief is neglecting the obligatory prayers."[35]

---

34 *Al-Bukhari*, # 1399.

35 *Muslim*, # 82-134.

Hypocrites also offer the obligatory prayers, but only so they are not considered disbelievers. However, they are lethargic, and their prayers suffer from shortcomings. The following are some of the shortcomings that can be seen in their prayers:

1. Being lethargic and late

A believer pays heed to his prayers, observes them on time, comes to them willingly and performs other forms of worship with zeal. Allah says:

> And those who pay heed to their prayers. (Qur'an 23:9)

The Prophet (ṣ) would wake up for the prayer with zeal. Someone asked 'Aishah when he would wake up for the prayer, and she said, "When he heard the cock crow, he would get up and offer the prayer."[36] According to another tradition, "He woke up with a yearning." He offered the *tahajjud* prayer and never exhibited laziness. Sa'id Ibn al-Musayyib said that for forty years, when the *'adhan* for the *fajr* prayer was called, he was already in the Masjid al-Nabawi.

Allah says about the hypocrites:

---

36 *Muslim*, # 131-741.

> The hypocrites think they are over-reaching Allah, but He will over-reach them. And when they stand up for prayer, they stand up lazily; they do it to be seen. Little do they hold Allah in remembrance. (Qur'an 4:142)

> That they come not to offer the prayer but sluggishly, and that they expend not but unwillingly. (Qur'an 9:54)

Anas Ibn Malik said that he heard Allah's Messenger (ṣ) say, "This is the hypocrite's prayer: he sits waiting for the sun (to set) and, when it is between the two horns of the devil (and turns yellow), he rises and offers the four *rak'ah*s, making little mention (of Allah) therein."[37]

The version in *Abu Dawud* says that he repeated "This is the hypocrite's prayer" three times and said that the hypocrite sits till the sun turns yellow.[38]

2. Offering prayer in a hurry

The believers are humble and attentive in their prayers.

---

37 *Kitab al-Zuhd*, pp. 458-459.

38 *Abu Dawud*, # 413.

> Prosperous indeed are the believers, those who in their prayers are humble. (Qur'an 23:1-2)

Without humbleness and attentiveness, the prayer earns no rewards. Rifa'ah Ibn Rafi' said that while they were seated around Allah's Messenger in the mosque one day, a man, who seemed to be a villager, came in, faced the *qiblah* and offered two *rak'ah*s of prayer. His prayer was very light: he did not perfect his bowing or prostrating. When he finished, he came and greeted the Prophet (ṣ) and the people (around him). The Prophet (ṣ) returned his greeting and said, "Go and offer the prayer, for you have not offered it." So he went and repeated what he had done before as Allah's Messenger (ṣ) observed his prayer intently. The man did not know what was wrong with his prayer. When he finished his prayer, he came again and greeted Allah's Messenger (ṣ) and the people around him. The Prophet (ṣ) returned his greeting as before and said, "But go and offer the prayer, for you have not offered it." So he repeated it three times.[39]

If one does not calmly go through the positions of standing, bowing and prostrating, then his praying is like a hen pecking at the seeds spread on the ground.

---

39 *Al-Tirmidhi*, # 303.

In these times, some people make a symbolic bowing and prostration in prayer. We must be cautious lest our prayers be rejected and resemble those of the hypocrites, which are only to be seen by others so that they are not considered infidels. Allah says of such worshippers:

> Then woe to (such) performers of prayer, who are heedless of their prayers, to those who make a display and refuse (even) a small assistance (to others). (Qur'an 107:4-7)

They are worshippers yet they face destruction. Their prayers are prayers in name only.

3. To regard prayer as a burden

To stay away from the prayer is a practice of hypocrites. The Prophet (ṣ) said, "By Him in whose hand is my soul, I resolved to give instructions for wood to be gathered, then for the prayer for which the *adhan* may be called. Then I would command a man to lead the people (in prayer) and I would go after the men (who stay away from the prayer) and burn down their homes over them. By Him in whose hand is my soul, were any of them to know that he would find a fat, meaty bone or a pair of good sheep hoofs, he would surely come to the *'isha'* prayer!"[40]

He also said, "The most burdensome prayer for the hypocrite is the *'isha'* and *fajr* prayers. If they knew what is given (in reward) for them, then they would come to them even if they had to drag themselves. Indeed, I resolved to command for the prayer to begin and for a man to lead the others. Then I would go with some men carrying with them dry wood to the people who did not attend the prayer, and I would burn down their homes over them with fire.[41]

According to another tradition, he said, "Were it not for the women and children in the homes, I would begin the *'isha'* prayer and command my young men to burn down with fire whatever is in the homes (of those who did not attend the prayer)."[42]

He only abstained from doing so because of the women and children, as attending the congregational prayers is not obligatory for them.

---

40 *Al-Bukhari*, # 644.

41 *Al-Bukhari*, #657.

42 *Ahmad*, #8441.

Moreover, whoever exits the mosque after the *adhan* and does not return is a hypocrite. Allah's Messenger (ṣ) said, "Whoever hears the call in this mosque of mine and goes out to attend to a need without returning is nothing but a hypocrite." [43]

The hypocrites find the *fajr* and *'isha'* prayers burdensome because they are sleepy at these hours. Here lies the difference between the believer and the hypocrite. The former will wait for the *'isha'* prayer even till midnight. The Companions prayed the *'isha'* late into the night sometimes and the *fajr* just as dawn was setting in. If anyone of them was ill, two men carried him to the mosque. Ibn Mas'ud said, "I observed none of us failed to attend the prayer except the known hypocrite or a sick person. If he was sick, he walked between two men to come to the prayer."[44]

4. Failing to pray the Friday prayer three times

Allah has made the Friday prayer obligatory for Muslims in order to train and purify them, to remind them about Islamic commands and knowledge of the

---

43 Al-Asbahani, *Sifah al-Nifaq*, #60.

44 *Muslim*, #654-256.

Shari'ah and to give them admonition and advice. Allah says:

> O you who believe, when the call is made for the (congregational) prayer on Friday, hasten to the remembrance of Allah and leave off your trading. That is better for you if you know. (Qur'an 62:9)

A Muslim is careful to observe the Friday prayer and keeps away from hypocrisy. One who misses three Friday prayers is recorded a hypocrite and Allah puts a seal on his heart. The Prophet (ṣ) said, "People must not miss their Friday prayers, otherwise Allah will place a seal on their hearts. Then they will become those who are neglectful."

The Prophet (ṣ) also said, "He who misses three Friday prayers without an excuse will be recorded among the hypocrites."

Now imagine someone who does not pray the Friday prayer at all. What kind of seal would be over his heart?

5. Making little mention of Allah

> Allah commands us to make much mention of him: The men who remember Allah much and the women who remember—Allah has prepared

> forgiveness and a great reward for them. (Qur'an 33:35)

As for the hypocrites, they make little mention of Allah:

> When they stand up for prayer, they stand up lazily, to be seen by (other) people, and they remember not Allah but a little. (Qur'an 4:142)

The Prophet (ṣ) said, "He who remembers Allah often is indeed free of hypocrisy."[45] He also said, "Shall I not inform you of the best of your deeds, the purest of them in the sight of your Master, the highest of your degrees, the one that is better for you than spending gold and silver, and better for you than your encountering the enemy and cutting off their heads and their cutting off yours?" The Companions said, "Of course." He said, "(It is) the remembrance of Allah Most High."[46]

Many traditions speak of the merits of remembrance of Allah. A believer's tongue must always be engaged in it. One of the Companions said to the Prophet (ṣ), "O Messenger of Allah, the laws of

---

45 Al-Asbahani, *Sifah al-Nifaq*, # 170.

46 *Al-Tirmidhi*, # 3437.

Islam overwhelm me, so give me some advice that I can adhere to." He said, "Always keep your tongue wet with the remembrance of Allah."[47]

47 *Al-Tirmidhi*, # 3435.

CHAPTER 10

Ostentatious Worship

Ostentation is a blameworthy quality and a minor kind of polytheism. It annuls deeds that are done ostentatiously, and instead of earning a reward, it makes the doer liable to punishment. It is another sign of the hypocrite. Allah says:

> ... showing off to people, and do not remember Allah but a little. (Qur'an 4:142)

Indeed, even worshippers will suffer ruin because of this trait.

> ... who (do good only to) show off. (Qur'an 107:6)

A hypocrite wants people to know that he offers the prayer, recites the Qur'an, gives charity, is very respectable, participates in *jihad* and observes fasting, but when he is by himself, he has nothing to do with religion. He perpetrates the forbidden when no one sees him.

The Prophet (ṣ) said, "I know a portion of my *ummah* who will come on the day of resurrection with deeds like the mountains of Tihamah (in hugeness). But, Allah will scatter their deeds like particles of dust in all directions." He was asked, "O Messenger of Allah, describe them to us. Make them well-known to us so that we may not be like them unknowingly." He said, "They are your brothers, of your own people. They are devoted to worship in the night as you are, but they are a people who, when alone, commit what Allah has forbidden."[48]

Hell will be fuelled by three kinds of people: those who did anything to show off as *mujahids*, reciters of the Qur'an or philanthropists. Though they are doers of highly rewarded deeds, their intentions were insincere and their acts ostentatious.

---

48 *Ibn Majah*, # 4245.

Kinds of ostentation

A *mujahid* may hope to earn a name for himself by taking part in *jihad*. A reciter of the Qur'an or a scholar may aim at receiving people's acclamation or want their names in large print in advertisements of meetings and gatherings. A philanthropist imagines that other people will speak of him as a kind-hearted, generous person.

If all these things are done to gain Allah's pleasure and there is no desire at all to be noticed and applauded, then there is no harm, even if the doer becomes famous.

The Prophet (ṣ) said, "If a person makes his doings heard, Allah will make his (evil) intention heard, and if he shows off, Allah will make him be seen (with his intention).[49]

This showing-off is a kind of minor polytheism. The Prophet (ṣ) said, "What I fear most for you is minor polytheism." He was asked, "O Messenger of Allah, what is it?" He said, "Ostentation. Allah will say on the Day of Resurrection, when He rewards the

---

49 *Al-Bukhari*, # 6499.

people for their deeds, 'Go to those whom you showed (your deeds) in the world, and see if you find with them a reward.'"[50]

Allah leaves the person with his ostentatious deeds and polytheism. The Prophet (ṣ) said, "On the Day of Resurrection, Allah will say, 'I am unconcerned with the association of partners. Whoever associated anything with Me in any deed will be abandoned by Me, as will the ones he associated (with Me).'"[51]

We must do everything we can to shun ostentation. The moment a person wishes to be known, he begins to do deeds for them to see. If he was humble for Allah's sake, Allah would raise him. The Prophet (ṣ) said, "No one is humble without Allah raising him."[52]

The hypocrite must realize that his deeds will be wasted if he does them to be seen, and it will amount to associating others with Allah. Only Allah can reward or punish. No one else can do that.

---

50 *Ahmad*, # 22523.

51 *Muslim*, # 46-2985.

52 *Muslim*, # 29-2588.

Nevertheless, a person may do his utmost to avoid associating anything with Allah but still fail. For this the Prophet (ṣ) taught us the following prayer:

"O Allah I seek refuge in You lest I associate (anything) with You knowingly, and I seek Your forgiveness for that which I do not know."[53]

---

53 *Ahmad*, 4/403.

Chapter 11

The Reciters of the Qur'an Are More Prone to Hypocrisy

Allah's Messenger (ṣ) said, "Most of the hypocrites in my *ummah* will be its reciters of the Qur'an."[54] Imam Ibn Athir explained it thus: "They try to ward off blame by memorizing the Qur'an while their intention is to remove it. This was what the hypocrites did in the time of the Prophet (ṣ).[55]

Many people memorise the Qur'an and get the word '*Hafiz*' appended before their names. They no longer ensure that they have the Qur'an preserved in their memory. But, the '*Hafiz*' is retained.

54 Al-Asbahani, *Sifah al-Nifaq*, # 155.

55 *Al-Nihayah fi Gharib Hadith wa al-Athar*, 4/31.

Chapter 12

Not Remembering Allah

A believer remembers Allah always. The Prophet (ṣ) said, "Allah Most High says, 'I am as My slave thinks of Me, and I am with him when he remembers Me. If he remembers Me secretly, I remember him secretly, and if he remembers Me among people, I remember him among a company better than them. If he draws near Me a span, I draw near him a cubit's length. If he draws near Me a cubit's length, I draw near him the length of two cubits. And if he comes to Me walking, I go to him running.'"[56]

However, the hypocrite forgets Allah, and if he remembers Him, it is very little.

Hypocrites, both men and women, are of one

56 *Al-Bukhari*, # 7405, 7505, 7537.

> another. They enjoin the wrong and forbid the right, and they withhold their hands (from expending for the cause of Allah). They forgot Allah, so He has forgotten them. Surely the hypocrites are the transgressors. (Qur'an 9:67)

> Satan has gained mastery over them, so he has made them forget the remembrance of Allah. Those are Satan's party. Behold, surely Satan's party are the losers! (Qur'an 58:19)

The hypocrite, like the infidel, concentrates on this world, his family, his skills. This is because his faith in the hereafter is not well-grounded.

To be disobedient to Allah and His Messenger

Believers never fail to obey Allah and His Messenger (ṣ), whatever difficulty that may entail. Allah says:

> The answer of the believers when they are called to Allah and to His Messenger so that he may judge between them is "We hear, and we obey." Such are the successful. (Qur'an 24:51)

In contrast, the hypocrite is occasionally obedient and very often he ignores Allah's commands. Allah says:

> And they swear by Allah their most earnest oaths

> that if you command them, they would certainly go forth. Say, "Do not swear. Known obedience (is better). Surely Allah is aware of what you do. (Qur'an 24:53)

Abu Umamah al-Bahili said, "When the hypocrite speaks, he lies; when he promises, he breaks it; when he is entrusted something, he betrays his trust; when he collects the spoils, he is treacherous; when he is commanded; he disobeys; and when he encounters (the enemy), he shows cowardice. So whoever has these traits has hypocrisy, and whoever has some of them has some hypocrisy."[57]

---

57 Al-Faryabi, *Sifah al- Nifaq*, # 20.

CHAPTER 13
To Ridicule People

To ridicule Muslims is the practice of hypocrites. As mentioned in the Qur'an, the hypocrites did this even in the Prophet's time. Ridicule can take a variety of forms:

1. Taunting those who do religious work

Muslims were in dire need of monetary help during the battle of Tabuk. When the Prophet (ṣ) appealed for a contribution, Abu Bakr brought everything he possessed, 'Umar brought his possessions and 'Uthman donated hundreds of well-equipped camels for Allah's cause. The Prophet (ṣ) remarked that if 'Uthman did nothing after that, then that single deed of his was enough. Some of the Companions engaged in manual labour and contributed their wages to the cause. But, instead of spending for this cause, the hypocrites made fun of the Muslims. Allah says about them:

> They who taunt those of the faithful who give their alms freely, and those who give to the extent of their earnings and scoff at them, will be paid back their scoffing by Allah and will have a painful chastisement. (Qur'an 9:79)

Abu Mas'ud said about this verse, "When we were commanded to give charity, we were labourers. Abu 'Aqil came with half a *sa'* (of dates), and another man ('Abd al-Rahman Ibn 'Awf) brought more than that. The hypocrites exclaimed, 'Surely Allah is in no need of this charity, and this second one has not done it but to show off.' This verse (Qur'an 9:79) was then revealed."[58]

There are people today who make fun of Muslims who adhere to the dictates of Islam, give charity, incline to piety, offer the prayer, dress according *Shari'ah*, grow the beard and take part in *jihad*. If a woman uses the veil, they taunt her and say that these are old-fashioned people. They consider themselves modern. But they will not hear anything against the

58 *Al-Bukhari*, # 1415.

disbelievers, who are their ideal.

Muslims should be careful of these people. Disbelievers do not cause harm to Muslims as much as these people.

2. Making fun of the Qur'an and *Sunnah*

With the increase of hypocrisy in him, the hypocrite finds Islamic ordinances and teachings a burden and begins to abandon them and make fun of them. He cares not for the Qur'an, the *Sunnah*, the pious or the hereafter. He has a plethora of excuses.

The hypocrites in the Prophet's time used to pray the prayer with him, fast, make the pilgrimage, pay the *zakah* and even wage *jihad* with him. When they did something wrong, Allah bracketed their evil with disbelief, saying:

> And if you question them, then they will certainly say, "We were only jesting and playing." Say, "Was it then at Allah and His revelations and His Messenger that you have been mocking? Make no excuses. You have indeed disbelieved after your belief. If we forgive a party of you, we shall chastise another party because they have been sinners." (Qur'an 9:65-66)

This verse was revealed during the battle of Tabuk concerning the hypocrites. It's context can be found in a tradition of 'Abdullah Ibn 'Umar, who said "A man participating in the battle of Tabuk said to a gathering, 'I have not seen anyone like these reciters of the Qur'an more lying with their tongues, more cowardly in the face of the enemy.' Another man ejaculated, 'You lie. Rather, you are a hypocrite. Indeed, I will inform Allah's Messenger (about it).' So that was conveyed to Allah's messenger and the Qur'an was revealed. I later saw him hanging by the rope of the Prophet's she-camel, the stones having wounded his feet and he was pleading, "O Messenger of Allah, we were merely jesting and playing." Allah's Messenger said, "Was it Allah and His verses and His Messenger that you made fun of? Make no excuses. You became disbelievers after you professed faith. If we forgive some of you, we shall punish some others because they were guilty."[59]

In a second incident regarding Qur'an 9:65, Qatadah said, "While the Prophet (ṣ) was engaged in the battle of Tabuk and a unit of the hypocrites was ahead of him, they said, 'He presumes that he will

---

59 *Tafsir Ibn Kathir*, Sūrah al-Tawbah: 65-66.

conquer the castles of Rome and its forts. Away, away!" Allah let his Prophet (ṣ) know of what they were saying. So he said, "It is incumbent on me to reckon with these people," and he summoned them and disclosed to them what they had been saying. They swore, 'We were only jesting and playing.'"

We must remember that to make fun of anything concerning religion is a sign of hypocrisy, be it the veil, the beard, clothes or *jihad*. The person doing it is an infidel. This is what the verse says. This conclusion can be drawn from the tradition of 'Abdullah Ibn 'Umar. [60]

3. Jokes and negative comment about a Muslim's honour

Hypocrites always try to tarnish a Muslim's reputation. They criticize and backbite about Muslims, though a proper Muslim is someone from whose hand and tongue others are safe.

'Abdullah Ibn Ubayy Ibn Salul, chief of the hypocrites, told his henchmen during a battle that they should not spend anything on the Companions of

60 *Al-Bukhari*, # 11, 6484.

Allah's Messenger (ṣ) till they deserted him. But later, when asked to explain, he denied that he had said anything. The verses of *Sūrah* al-Munafiqin (Qur'an 63:7-8) were then revealed and his mischief was brought to light. These verses were presented earlier in the chapter on falsehood. The hypocrites made fun of the Muslims. Allah says:

> And when they meet those who believe, they say, "We believe," and when they are alone with their devils, they say, "Surely we are with you; we were only mocking (them)." Allah mocks them and leaves them wandering blindly in their contumacy. (Qur'an 2:14-15)

CHAPTER 14

Abusing Others

Allah's Messenger (ṣ) said,

> "A believer does not taunt, does not revile, is not immoral and is not shameless."[61]

The Prophet (ṣ) also said that if anyone possesses four things, then he is a hypocrite, and one of these is that he abuses when he quarrels.

While it is allowed to avenge an abuse, it is not allowed to lie. The Prophet (ṣ) said,

> "When two men revile one another, whatever they say is against the first one as long as the one wronged does not transgress (in seeking

61. *Al-Tirmidhi*, # 1977.

> revenge)."[62]

If the one wronged lies against the initiator, then both are hypocritical. The Prophet (ṣ) said,

> "Two people who revile one another are both devilish, abusers and liars."[63]

But if one of them endures patiently, then it is good for him. Allah says:

> Whosoever defends himself after he has been wronged—against such there is no cause of blame. (Qur'an 42:41)
>
> Indeed if any shows patience and forgives, that would only be an exercise of courageous will and resolution in the conduct of affairs. (Qur'an 42:43)

---

62. *Muslim*, # 68-2587.

63. *Al-Targhib wa al-Tarhib*, # 4207.

CHAPTER 15

To Forbid Piety and Enjoin Evil

It is a religious duty to enjoin piety and forbid evil. If anyone neglects this duty, he commits a sin. The Prophet (ṣ) said, "By Him in whose hand is my soul, either you enjoin good and forbid evil or Allah will soon send you a punishment from Him, after which you will pray to Him but He will not respond to you."[64]

When the children of Israel forsook this duty, they were cursed by Prophet Dawud and 'Isa, son of Maryam.

> Cursed were those who disbelieved from among the children of Israel by the tongue of Dawud and of 'Isa, son of Maryam. That was because they

---

64 *Al-Tirmidhi*, # 2169.

> disobeyed and used to transgress the limits. (Qur'an 5:78)

If neglecting duties is punishable, then imagine the reward for doing the opposite—for enjoining or promoting evil and preventing or forbidding piety. If anyone does not recognize evil, then his heart is devoid of faith. The Prophet (ṣ) said, "If any of you sees evil (being done), he must prevent it with his hand. If he is unable to do so, then (he must prevent it) with his tongue. If he is unable to do that, then (he must regard it as evil) in his heart—and that is the weakest form of faith."[65]

If the heart is devoid of faith, then disbelief or hypocrisy resides therein. Hence, Allah describes it as a hypocrite's character.

> Hypocrites, both men and women, are of one another. They enjoin the wrong and forbid the right, and they withhold their hands (from expending in the way of Allah). They forgot Allah, so He has forgotten them. Surely the hypocrites are the transgressors. (Qur'an 9:67)

Preventing piety may take various forms, such

---

65 *Muslim*, # 78-49.

mocking someone who offers the prayer, not permitting a servant to pray, not permitting someone to take part in *jihad* and speaking against it, not fasting and ridiculing those who do, and discouraging others from building mosques or *madrasahs*.

Enjoying evil also takes different forms. One may invite others to watch indecent movies or television shows, to tease women, to encourage the customs of evil people, to advocate an evil social life, to discourage the *hijab*, to say the *hijab* is only of the heart or the eyes, to sell intoxicants, to circulate immoral magazines or to spread immodesty through print media.

To promote immodesty, to listen to frivolous songs and to tease women and girls

Those people who try to promote and spread immodesty among Muslims are hypocrites. Allah says:

> Surely for those who love that indecency should be spread concerning those who believe will be a painful chastisement in this world and the hereafter. Allah knows, while you know not. (Qur'an 24:19)

This verse makes it clear that spreading indecency

through videos, films, musical instruments, dances, songs and the like are all hypocritical deeds. Whoever is involved in them invites divine punishment.

> Of mankind is he who buys frivolous discourse to lead astray (others) from Allah's way without knowledge, and to take it in mockery. For them is a humiliating chastisement. (Qur'an 31:6)

Regarding the words "frivolous discourse," 'Abdullah Ibn Mas'ud said, "By Allah, they refer to singing."[66]

To tease girls

It is again the hypocrite who will tease the women and girls he comes across. In the time of the Prophet (ṣ), men would station themselves on street corners and tease passing women. When they were reprimanded, they put forward the pretext that they did not know if the women were slaves or free, respectable ladies. So Allah ordained:

> O Prophet, say to your wives and your daughters and the women of the believers to draw their outer garments close round them. In this way, it is more

---

66 *Al-Tabari*, 20/127.

> probable that they will be recognized and not annoyed. Allah is forgiving, merciful. (Qur'an 33:59)

Allah warned the hypocrites:

> Indeed if the hypocrites and those in whose hearts is a disease and those who stir up sedition in Madinah desist not, We shall most surely give you authority over them. Then they will not be your neighbours therein except for a while. (Qur'an 33:60)

The chief of the hypocrites, 'Abdullah Ibn Ubayy, earned money by coercing his female slaves into prostitution. Allah made known his filthy deed and forbade others from doing evil.

> Force not your slave girls into prostitution if they desire to keep chaste, so that you may seek the enjoyment of the life of this world. (Qur'an 24:33)

Clearly, Muslims prefer to live chaste lives and only the hypocrites promote indecency. Many people find excuses to make adultery prevalent in society. Their character resembles that of hypocrites.

CHAPTER 16

To Behave Shamelessly

Modesty and decency are two blessings that keep a person away from evil. When these two are absent, one is willing to do every wrong. The Prophet (ṣ) said, "One of the sayings of early prophets that has reached people is 'When you do not feel ashamed, do whatever you like.'"[67]

Believers possess modesty. Sa'd Ibn 'Ubadah said that if he were to see a stranger with his wife, he would strike him with his sword. When the Prophet (ṣ) heard of this, he said, "Are you surprised at Sa'd's sense of modesty? I have a greater sense of it than he, and Allah has a greater one than I."[68]

---

67 *Al-Bukhari*, # 6120.

68 *Al-Bukhari*, # 7416

The hypocrite, on the other hand, likes indecency and shamelessness. He lacks a sense of modesty. The Prophet (ṣ) said, "Modesty and little speech are branches of faith, while obscenity and talkativeness are branches of hypocrisy."[69] He also (ṣ) said, "Modesty is part of faith, while immodesty is part of hypocrisy."

These things are very common today and can be found in nearly every home. Our weddings are gatherings of unveiled women who move about among men unconcerned, and their videos are made without compunction. This is hypocritical and shameless.

To commit sin fearlessly when alone

The Qur'an repeatedly tells us that a believer fears Allah. He fears Him whether or not he is alone. He is convinced that Allah sees him and he will have to account for all his deeds, minor and major, before Allah on the Day of Resurrection.

The hypocrite does good deeds only to be seen by other people. When he is alone, he is fearless and commits sin because he lacks the conviction in the

69 *Al-Tirmidhi*, # 2027

hereafter. Allah says:

> And there are some who say, "We believe in Allah and the Last Day" while they are not believers (in fact). (Qur'an 2:8)

> They seek to conceal from people, but they cannot conceal from Allah, for He is with them when by night they plan together a discourse which pleases Him not. And Allah ever encompasses what they do. (Qur'an 4:10)

The Prophet (ṣ) said, "I know a portion of my *Ummah* who will come on the Day of Resurrection with deeds like the mountains of Tihamah (in huge piles). But Allah will scatter them like particles of dust in every direction." Thawban (the narrator) asked him to describe them to them so that they might be careful. He said, "They are your brothers, of your own people. They devote themselves to worship in the night as you do, but when they are alone they commit that which Allah has forbidden.[70]

This is a sign of the hypocrites who are seen to worship much, but in private commit many sins. A hypocrite dislikes piety and is not afraid of

---

70 *Ibn Majah*, # 4245.

punishment for sins.

When ‘Umar Ibn al-Khattab went to the Levant, he addressed the people. After praising Allah and glorifying Him, he said, “Allah’s Messenger stood among us to preach, just as I have stood among you today, and said, The sign of the hypocrite is that evil does not hurt him and piety does not please him. If he does a good deed, he does not hope to receive a reward for that good deed from Allah. And if he does a bad deed, he does not fear a punishment from Allah for that bad deed.”[71]

Bilal Ibn Sa‘d said, “Do not become a friend of Allah in public and His enemy in private.”[72]

Cowardice and foreboding

A Muslim never displays cowardice. This is why Allah has said that those who show their backs in battle will be severely punished.

He says:

O you who believe, when you encounter those who

---

71 *Sifah al-Nifaq*, # 67.

72 Al-Faryabi, *Sifah al- Nifaq*, # 91.

> disbelieve marching to battle, turn not your backs to them. Whoever turns his back that day to them, unless manoeuvring for battle or turning to join a host (of his own), incurs wrath from Allah, and his abode is Hell—an evil destination. (Qur'an 8:15-16)

The hypocrites are cowards and fear the vicissitudes of time. They also instil this fear in others and think every tragedy is befalling them. Allah says:

> They think every shout is against them. (Qur'an 63:4)

Abu Umamah al-Bahili described a hypocrite as someone who lies when he speaks, breaches his promise when he makes one, betrays when he is entrusted, misappropriates when he gathers booty, disobeys when he is commanded and behaves cowardly when he encounters an enemy. Hence, whoever has these traits is a hypocrite, and whoever has some of these has that much of hypocrisy in him.

Allah says:

> And they swear by Allah that they are truly of you, whereas they are not of you. But they are a people who are afraid. If they could find a refuge, or some caverns, or a place to enter, they would surely have resorted thereto hastily. (Qur'an 9:56-57)

When he is scared, the hypocrite sees death hovering over him, but when the fear recedes, he does not tire boasting about his bravery. Allah says:

> Being covetous over you. But when fear comes, you will see them looking at you, their eyes rolling like someone who swoons of death. But when the fear is gone, they smite you with sharp tongues, being covetous of the best (of spoils). These (hypocrites) have not believed, so Allah makes their deeds to fail—that is easy for Allah. (Qur'an 33:19)

Abu Talhah said, "On the day of Uhud, drowsiness overtook us while we were in battle rows. My sword dropped down from my hand. I picked it up and it dropped again, and again I picked it up. The other party was that of the hypocrites, who had no concern at all but for themselves, the most cowardly of people, the most frightened, fleeing from the truth.

> 'They thought wrongly of Allah, the thought of ignorance' (Qur'an 3:154).

They lie and doubt Allah's affairs."

Chapter 17

To Eulogise a Ruler to His Face but Criticise Him behind His Back

Abu Sha'tha' said, "Some people from Iraq went to 'Abdullah Ibn 'Umar and launched into a tirade against Yazid Ibn Mu'awiyah, speaking ill of him. 'Abdullah Ibn 'Umar asked them whether they had said the same to his face. They confessed, 'No. Rather, we praise him to his face.' Ibn 'Umar told them that they considered this conduct hypocrisy."[73]

An imam against a petition gives a wicked decision and we say to him, "May Allah enable you (to do justice)." But we also observe one of us shower praise on him. Ibn 'Umar said, "We are a company of the Companions of Allah's Messenger and we

73 Al-Faryabi, *Sifah al- Nifaq*, # 67.

consider this hypocrisy. But I cannot say how you people classify it."[74]

74 Al-Asbahani, *Sifah al-Nifaq*, #94.

CHAPTER 18

Miserliness

Allah commands us to spend for His cause and encourages us to go on doing that. We find many examples of liberal spending by the Companions. Allah says:

> And expend for the cause of Allah, cast not yourselves by your own hands into ruin, and do good. Allah loves the good doers. (Qur'an 2:195)

He says about miserliness:

> Those who are niggardly, and enjoin niggardliness on others, and hide the bounties which God had bestowed on them, for we have prepared for those who resist faith, a punishment that steeps them in contempt. (Qur'an 4:37)

And also,

> And as for those who are niggardly in expending

> that which Allah has granted them out of His bounty, let them not think that it is good for them. Nay, it is bad for them. Soon will that in which they were niggardly be hung round their necks on the Day of Resurrection. To Allah belongs the heritage of the heavens and the earth. Allah is aware of what you do. (Qur'an 3:180)

A believer is never miserly. It is the hypocrite who is miserly. Allah says:

> And of them are some who have made a covenant with Allah (saying), "If He gives us out of His bounty, we will certainly give alms and be of the righteous. Yet when He gave them of His bounty, they became niggardly of it and turned away while they were averse. (Qur'an 9:75-76)

It is not proper to compel anyone to spend for Allah's cause. It is also wrong to force someone to increase his spending for Allah's cause.

Chapter 19

To Scare People by Spreading Rumours

A Muslim does not spread rumours or cause panic. This is, in fact, a sign of the hypocrite.

> Indeed, if the hypocrites and those in whose hearts there is a disease and those who circulate sedition in Madinah desist not, we shall most surely give you authority over them. Then they will not be your neighbours therein except for a while. (Qur'an 33:60)

When the hypocrites go anywhere with the Muslims be it a battle or any other purpose, their conduct is depicted in this verse:

> Had they gone forth with you, they would have increased you in nothing but trouble, and would have hurried to and fro in your midst, seeking to stir up sedition among you. Among you there are some who would have listened to them. Allah

> knows well the evildoers. (Qur'an 9:47)

"Trouble" here includes panic and tale-bearing against Muslims, causing a rift among them. They also give wrong advice. A hypocrite spreads rumours to cause Muslims to lose courage and feel dejected. He spreads false news by exaggerating the figures of their casualties and the strength of the enemies. But one should remember that strength lies in Allah's hands, and none can overcome whoever Allah helps.

> And there is no help except from Allah. (Qur'an 3:126)

> If Allah helps you, there is none who can overcome you. (Qur'an 3:160)

As for those who get support from the infidels, Allah says:

> The parable of those who take protectors other than Allah is that of the spider that makes a house, and most surely the frailest of houses is the spider's house—if they only knew. (Qur'an 29:41)

To spread mischief on Earth

Islam gives Muslims a society of peace and security. It protects life, property and honour. It has prescribed punishments for those who try to disturb the peace.

Allah says:

> The only recompense of those who wage war against Allah and His Messenger and strive to do corruption in the land is that they should be slain or crucified, their hands and feet cut should be cut off on opposite sides or they should be banished from the land. That is a degradation for them in this world, and in the hereafter awaits them a mighty chastisement. (Qur'an 5:33)

The Prophet (ṣ) said, "The Muslim is one from whose tongue and hands other Muslims are safe."[75]

Hypocrites spread mischief on earth. They murder innocent people, destroy fields and kill animals. Allah says:

> Of mankind there is he whose talk about the life of this world pleases you, and he calls on Allah to witness as to that which is in his heart, yet he is the most stubborn in altercation. And when he turns back, he makes effort in the land to do corruption therein and to destroy the tillage and the stock, and Allah loves not corruption. And when it is said to him, "Fear Allah," arrogance seizes him in sin, so Hell will be enough for him, and it is certainly an

75 *Al-Bukhari*, # 10

evil resting place. (Qur'an 2:204-206)

Had they gone forth with you, they would have increased you in nothing but trouble, and would have hurried to and fro in your midst, seeking to stir up sedition among you. Among you there are some who would have listened to them. Allah knows well the evildoers. (Qur'an 9:47)

When it is said to them, "Do not do corruption on the earth," they say, "We are only peacemakers." Beware! Surely they are the corrupters, but they perceive it not. (Qur'an 2:11-12)

Many people harm religion in the name of progress and resort to polytheism and innovations.

Then, is it to be expected of you, if you were put in authority, that you would do mischief in the land and break your ties of kith and kin? (Qur'an 47:22)

Chapter 20

To Desire to See Muslims Suffering

A Muslim wishes well for his fellow Muslim. He neither deserts him nor hurts him. To curse anyone or wish for his suffering is also to hurt him. The Prophet (ṣ) said. Be, O slaves of Allah, brothers to one another. A Muslim is a Muslim's brother. He does not hurt him nor desert him nor belittle him. Righteousness is here (pointing to his chest)."[76]

A hypocrite always wishes for the suffering of Muslims. But when Muslims gain victory, he assures them that he belongs to their ranks. Allah says:

> If there be a victory for you from Allah, those who wait about you (for something to happen) say, "Were we not with you?" And if there be some

76 *Muslim*, # 2564-32.

> share (of success) for the disbelievers, they say (to them), "Did we not have control over you, yet we defended you against the believers?" So Allah will judge between you on the Day of Resurrection. Allah will not give the disbelievers a way against the believers. (Qur'an 4:141)

Allah also says,

> And of the desert Arabs are some who take what they expend as a loss and await for an (evil) turn of fortune for you. On them will be an evil turn of fortune. Allah hears and knows. (Qur'an 9:98)

Glib-tongued arrogance

Allah says about the hypocrites:

> They smite you with sharp tongues, being covetous of the best of (spoils). (Qur'an 33:19)

> And when you see them, their figures please you, and if they speak, you listen to their speech. (Yet) they are like propped-up beams of timber. They think every shout (they hear) to be against them. They are the enemy, so beware of them. May Allah destroy them! How they are perverted! (Qur'an 63:4)

The Prophet (ṣ) said, "Surely, the dearest of you to me and the nearest of you to me in company on the

Day of Resurrection will be the best of you in manners. And the most despised of you to me and the furthest away from me on the Day of Resurrection will be the talkative, the loud-mouthed (careless in speech) and the *mutafayhiqun*." The Companions said, "O Messenger of Allah, indeed we know who the talkative and loud-mouthed are. But who are the *mutafayhiqun*?" He said, "The arrogant."[77]

Allah does not like anyone to be arrogant. The Prophet (ṣ) said, "He will not enter Hell who has a mustard seed's weight of faith in his heart. And he will not enter paradise who has a mustard seed's weight of pride in his heart."[78]

According to a tradition, Allah says, "Majesty is My lower garment and pride is my cloak. Whoever tries to pull either one of them, I will indeed punish."[79]

The hypocrite is arrogant. Allah says:

> And when it is said to them, "Come; Allah's Messenger will ask forgiveness for you," they twist their heads and you see them turning away their

---

77 *Al-Tirmidhi*, # 2018.

78 *Muslim*, # 91-91-148.

79 *Muslim*, # 2620-136.

> faces while they show arrogance. (Qur'an 63:5)

To love infidels and despise Muslims

Muslims are brothers to one another. Allah says:

> The believers are but brethren. (Qur'an 49:10)

> And the believing men and the believing women are friends of one another. They enjoin the right and forbid the wrong, establish the prayer, pay the *zakah* and obey Allah and His Messenger. They are those on whom Allah will have mercy. Allah is mighty, wise. (Qur'an 9:71)

Allah's Messenger (ṣ) said, "Believers, in their compassion for each other, love for each other and kindness towards each other, are like a body. When a limb feels pain, the entire body loses sleep and runs a fever."[80]

Instead of showing love to Muslims, a hypocrite befriends infidels. Allah says,

> O you who believe, take not Jews and Christians as friends. They are friends of each other. And whosoever among you takes them as friends is indeed one of them. Surely Allah guides not evil-

80 *Al-Bukhari*, # 6011.

doing people. (Qur'an 5:51)

Hypocrites, both men and women, are of one another. They enjoin the wrong and forbid the right, and they withhold their hands (from expending for the cause of Allah). They forgot Allah, so He has forgotten them. Surely the hypocrites are the transgressors. (Qur'an 9:67)

Have you not considered those who have taken for friends a people with whom Allah is wroth. They are neither of you nor of them, and they swear to a lie while they know. Allah has prepared for them a severe chastisement. Surely vile is what they have been doing. (Qur'an 58:14-15)

Give hypocrites glad tidings of a painful punishment for them. Do those who take disbelievers for their friends instead of believers seek honour through them? Surely, honour is Allah's altogether. (Qur'an 4:138-139)

O you who believe, take not intimates other than your own people. They spare no pains to ruin you. They love that which vexes you. Hatred has indeed already appeared from their mouths, and that which their hearts conceal is yet greater. We have indeed made plain to you the revelations if you understand. Ah! You are those who love them, but they love you not, even though you believe in all

> the (revealed) books. When they meet you, they say, "We believe," and when they are alone, they bite their fingertips at you in rage. Say (to them), "Perish in your rage. Surely, Allah knows what is in hearts." (Qur'an 3:118-119)

These verses and traditions show how the hypocrite behaves: he inclines towards infidels. But only a Muslim considers Islam and faith, which ensure success both in this world and in the hereafter, instead of a mere temporal profit, which the materialistic way of life advocates.

To help further disbelief

If anyone aids in promoting disbelief, then he has both hypocrisy and disbelief. If infidels hurt Muslims because of someone's help, then he will be executed. Allah says:

> They long that you should disbelieve as they disbelieve so that you are at par (with them). Therefore take not friends from among them until they emigrate in Allah's way. But if they turn their backs (to emigration), seize them and slay them wherever you find them, and take not anyone of them as a friend or a helper. (Qur'an 4:89)

> O you who believe, take not Jews and Christians as

> friends. They are friends of each other. And whosoever among you takes them as friends is indeed one of them. Surely Allah guides not evil-doing people. (Qur'an 5:51)

Whoever disobeys Allah and supports them will be counted among them and will die as a disbeliever. Ibn 'Abbas said, "Some Muslims in the time of the Prophet (ṣ) joined the idolators, thus increasing their numbers. An arrow would be shot and hit one of them and kill him, or a sword would strike him and kill him. So Allah revealed,

> 'When angels take the souls of those who die in sin against their souls, they say, "In what (plight) were you?" They reply, "Weak and oppressed were we in the earth." They say, "Was not the earth of Allah spacious enough for you to move yourselves away (from evil)?" Such men find their abode in Hell—what an evil refuge' (Qur'an 4:97)."[81]

To rejoice at the distress of believers

A Muslim sympathises with his Muslim brother when he is in distress or difficulty. He exhorts him to be patient.

---

81 *Al-Bukhari*, # 4596.

Whenever, the Prophet (ṣ) visited anyone to condole with him, he would pray, "Surely, to Allah belongs what He has taken away and what He has given. Everything has an appointed time with Him. So you must be patient and seek a reward (from Him)."[82]

Hypocrites rejoice when Muslims face a difficulty, but if Muslims gain something, hypocrites become depressed and jealous, hoping that whatever they gained will be taken away.

> If some good fortune visits you, it vexes them, and if evil befalls you, they rejoice at it. But if you persevere and fear (Allah), their guile will not harm you in any way. Surely Allah encompasses what they do. (Qur'an 3:120)

> If success betides you, it will grieve them, and if a reverse overtakes you, they will say (to themselves), "We were careful to protect our affair in advance." And they turn away, rejoicing. (Qur'an 9:50)

But Allah says to them,

> Say, "Nothing can befall us except that which Allah has prescribed for us. He is our protector, and in Allah let believers put their trust." Say, "Do you expect for us anything other than the two best

---

82 *Al-Bukhari*, # 1284.

> things? But we expect for you that Allah will afflict you with chastisement from Him or at our hands. So await; we too are awaiting with you." (Qur'an 9:51-52)

If, in His wisdom, Allah tries Muslims with an affliction and spares hypocrites, they boast that they knew what would happen and that they were prepared for it. They will pretend to sympathise, but will rejoice inwardly.

To stay away when Muslims are in distress, and to associate with them when they are not

Allah says:

> And surely among you here is he who lags behind. if misfortune befalls you, he says, "Allah has blessed me in that I was not present with them." But if bounty from Allah reaches you, he certainly cries, as if there had never been any affection between you and him, "Would that I had been with them, then I would have attained a mighty triumph. (Qur'an 4:72-73)

If anyone faces hardship because of abiding by Islamic teachings, then hypocrites attribute that to Allah's punishment. Rather, this is a trial and it sifts the genuine from the fake. Allah says,

> And among people is he who says, "We believe in Allah," but if he is made to suffer for the sake of Allah, he takes the persecution of people as if it were Allah's chastisement. Then if help comes from your Lord, they say, "Surely we were with you." Does not Allah know best what is in the hearts of (His) creatures? Allah will certainly determine those who believe, and He will certainly determine the hypocrites. (Qur'an 29:10-11)

It is also the characteristic of the hypocrites that they will hasten to join the Muslims to receive a share in the booty that the Muslims acquire.

> Those who were left behind will soon say, "When you set forth to take spoils, allow us to follow you." They desire to change the word of Allah. Say, "You will not go with us. Thus did Allah say before." Then they will say, "Nay, you are jealous of us." Nay, they understand only a little. (Qur'an 48:15)

A hypocrite will change sides between Muslims and non-Muslims according to where his advantage lies and the difficulties each side faces.

To do that which harms Islam

'Uqbah Ibn 'Amir said that he heard Allah's Messenger (ṣ) say, "The ruin of my ummah lies in the

Book (the Qur'an) and milk." Someone asked, "O Messenger of Allah, in the Book and milk?" He said, "They will learn the Qur'an and will interpret it in a way other than it was revealed. And they will love milk, forsake the congregational prayer and the Friday prayer and take to villages."[83]

Ibn Rajab explained this tradition, saying, "They will stay in villages as long as there is milk, and that is always a lengthy period. During this period, they will forsake Friday and congregational prayers."[84]

This is a sign of hypocrisy. We have stated earlier that if anyone misses three Friday prayers, then he is recorded as a hypocrite, and only a hypocrite keeps away from the congregational prayer. However, if congregational and Friday prayers are observed in the village and one does not neglect them then, there is no harm in going to the village. But Allah knows best.

---

83 *Ahmad*, # 16780.

84 *Fath al-Bari*, 1/108.

CHAPTER 21

To Bear Malice towards the Companions

The hypocrites bore malice towards the Companions. The Prophet (ṣ) said, "No one but a believer loves the Ansar and none but a hypocrite despises them. So whoever loves them, Allah loves, and whoever despises them, Allah despises."[85]

He also said, "A sign of hypocrisy is to hate the Ansar, and a sign of belief is to love them." [86]

To bear malice towards 'Ali is also hypocrisy. Zirr Ibn Hubaysh said, "I heard 'Ali say, 'By Him who pierced the grain, created the living and gave it bones,

---

85 *Al-Bukhari*, # 3783.

86 *Muslim*, # 74-128.

surely the Prophet (ṣ) had assured me that only a believer will love me and none but a hypocrite will hate me.'"[87]

Al-Dhahabi said, "To love 'Ali is faith and to hate him is hypocrisy. There are many branches of faith and many branches of hypocrisy. No sensible person will say that whoever loves 'Ali is a perfect believer and whoever hates him is a true hypocrite. Thus, whoever loves 'Ali but hates Abu Bakr is like someone who hates 'Ali but loves Abu Bakr. Hence, to hate either or both of them is to go astray and have hypocrisy, while love for both of them is guidance and faith.

To love all the Companions is a sign of faith and to bear malice towards any one of them for any reason is a sign of hypocrisy.

'Aishah said that she heard the Prophet (ṣ) say, when 'Uthman Ibn 'Affan came to him one night, "Allah will make you wear a shirt, and if the hypocrites intend to remove it, do not take it off till you meet me."[88]

---

87 *Sifah al-Nifaq*, # 71.

88 *Al-Tirmidhi*, # 3705

Chapter 22

Lack of Understanding the Religion

An understanding of religion is a great blessing of Allah. The Prophet (ṣ), "When Allah decides to let someone have good, He gives him an understanding of religion."[89] However, the hypocrite is deprived of religious knowledge and understanding, though he may have mastered worldly knowledge. Allah says:

> They know the outward appearance of the life of this world, but of the hereafter they are heedless. (Qur'an 30:7)

There are many instances in the Qur'an that prove that hypocrites have no religious knowledge or understanding. For example, Allah says:

> They are those who say, "Expend not on those who

---

89 *Al-Bukhari*, # 71.

> are with Allah's Messenger until they disperse." To Allah belong the treasures of the heavens and the earth, but the hypocrites understand not. They say, "If we return to Madinah, the mightier ones of it will expel there from the meaner ones." Might belongs to Allah and to His Messenger and believers, but the hypocrites know not. (Qur'an 63:7-8)

> They seek to deceive Allah and those who believe, whereas they deceive none but themselves, but they perceive not. (Qur'an 2:9)

> And when it is said to them, "Believe as (other) people have believed," they say, "Shall we believe as fools have believed?" Beware! Surely they are the foolish ones, but they know it not. (Qur'an 2:13)

In short, a hypocrite is unaware of religious knowledge. He may be proficient in worldly sciences and may even try to acquire them, but he lacks proficiency in religious sciences. Hypocrites cite the tradition that "it is obligatory for every Muslim to acquire knowledge" in support of acquiring worldly sciences, conveniently ignoring its real meaning: to gain divine awareness and knowledge of the Qur'an and *Sunnah*. While it is not disallowed to acquire worldly sciences, it is meaningless to acquire them without religious knowledge. Knowledge of religion is a means of success in the hereafter. Therefore it must be sought first.

CHAPTER 23

To Disbelieve the Promises of Allah and His Messenger (ṣ)

A believer does not disbelieve Allah's and His Prophet's promises. Allah says:

> And when the believers saw the confederates, they said, "This is what Allah and His Messenger promised us, and Allah and His Messenger spoke the truth." It only increased them in faith and submission. (Qur'an 33:22)

It is hypocrites who disbelieve promises. During the Battle of the Trenches, the Prophet (ṣ) was occupied with digging the trenches with his Companions when they encountered a stubborn rock, which the Prophet (ṣ) struck with his pickaxe. At each of his two strikes, a flash rose from it and he remarked, "I have been shown two treasures, both of which my *ummah* will receive." The hypocrites around the trench winked at each other, suggesting that while they were in the grip of fear, he raised in them expectations of the treasures of Caesar and Chosroes. Allah revealed this verse concerning them:

> And when the hypocrites and those in whose hearts was a disease were saying, "Allah and His Messenger promised us nothing but delusion." (Qur'an 33:12)

The hypocrites belied Allah's and His Prophet's (ṣ) promises. But Allah gave the Muslims a victory and disgraced the hypocrites.

> Allah makes other promises in the Qur'an. For example: Allah has promised to make those of you who believe and do righteous deeds successors on the earth, just as He made those before them successors, and to establish for them their religion, which He has approved for them, and to give them in exchange, after their fear, security. "They will worship Me, associating nothing with me." And those who disbelieve after this are the transgressors. (Qur'an 24:55)

Allah also assured the Muslims of His help if they helped His religion:

> O you who believe, if you help Allah, He will help you and make your feet firm. (Qur'an 47:7)

A Muslim never disbelieves any of the promises made by Allah or His Prophet (ṣ). Only a hypocrite would do such a horrible thing. A Muslim has complete faith in Allah, His Messenger (ṣ) and the *Shari'ah*.

Chapter 24

To Rely on Laws other than Shari'ah

Islam has prescribed certain punishments to keep the society in a peaceful working order and everyone may get his basic rights easily and justice may prevail. Allah has made the laws clear in the Qur'an. He says:

> The answer of the believers, when they are called to Allah and to His Messenger so that he may judge between them, is "We hear and we obey." Such are the successful. (Qur'an 24:51)

Hypocrites ignore the *Shari'ah* laws and obey the laws of the *taghut* (or false gods). Allah says about them:

> Have you not considered those who assert that they believe in what has been revealed to you, and what was revealed before you? (Yet) they desire to seek the judgement (of their disputes) from *taghut*,

> whereas they indeed have been commanded to disbelieve in them. But Satan desires to lead them astray into far error. When it is said to them, "Come now to that which Allah has revealed, and to the Messenger," you then see the hypocrites turn away from you with aversion. (Qur'an 4:60-61)

However, if hypocrites are confident of getting a favourable judgement from the *Shari'ah* court, then they profess unflinching obedience. Allah says:

> And when they are called to Allah and to His Messenger so that he may judge between them, behold, a party of them are averse. But if the right is on their side, they come to him submissively. Is there disease in their hearts, or are they in doubt, or do they fear that Allah and His Messenger will deal unjustly with them? Nay, those are the evildoers. (Qur'an 24:48-50)

Those who turn away from the *Shari'ah* in favour of the laws that suit them must ask themselves who they are: Muslims or hypocrites?

Those who do not judge by the Qur'an are sinners, transgressors and infidels. Allah says:

> And whosoever judges not by that which Allah has revealed are the disbelievers. (5:44)

... they are the evil doers. (Qur'an 5:45)

... they are the transgressors. (Qur'an 5:47)

CHAPTER 25

To Have Doubts about Predestination

It is part of faith to believe in predestination. When Jibril came to the Prophet (ṣ) in human form and asked some questions, he also asked, "Now, tell me about faith." He said, "That you believe in Allah, His angels, His revealed books, His messengers and the Last Day, and that you believe in destiny, both good and evil." He said, "You have spoken the truth."[90]

The Prophet (ṣ) also said, "A person does not believe unless he (also) believes in destiny, both of good and evil, till he is convinced that what has afflicted him could not have been averted and what has been averted could not have afflicted him."[91]

---

90 *Al-Bukhari*, # 1.

91 *Al-Tirmidhi*, # 2144.

> Allah says: Every affliction that befalls earth or yourselves is in a book before we bring it forth. Surely that is easy for Allah. (Qur'an 57:22)

Allah tries every Muslim in different ways to separate the persevering from the dissenters. On predestination He says:

> And we shall certainly try you with something of fear, hunger and loss of wealth, lives and fruits. Give glad tidings to the persevering, who, when affliction befalls them, say, "Surely, we belong to Allah, and to Him we are to return." Those are the ones on whom are blessings and mercy from their Lord, and those are the ones who are rightly guided. (Qur'an 2:155-157)

Thus, it is part of faith to believe in the decreeing of good and evil. If one does not believe in this, then one is not a Muslim

A hypocrite raises objections to the decreeing. This is exactly what the hypocrites did after the battle of Uhud, when seventy of the Companions were martyred. Allah says:

> Those who said of their brethren, while they themselves held back, "Had they obeyed us, they would not have been slain." Say, "Then avert death from yourselves if you are truthful." (Qur'an 2:168)

What is destined cannot be averted. Those who wail when afflicted quiet down in the end, but the perseverant are quiet from the beginning.

CHAPTER 26

To Spy on People

A Muslim is not allowed to spy on another Muslim. Spying on others is a major sin. Allah says:

> O you who believe, avoid much of suspicion, for surely some suspicion is a sin. And spy not, nor backbite one another. Would any one of you like to eat the flesh of his dead brother? So you would abhor that! And fear Allah. Surely, Allah is relenting, merciful. (Qur'an 49:12)

Al-Bara' Ibn 'Azib said that Allah's Messenger (ṣ) addressed them so that women also heard him within their veils. He called out in a loud voice, "O company of those who have believed with their tongues but in whose hearts faith has not been established sincerely, do not backbite about Muslims and do not seek to find their faults, for whoever seeks to find the faults of his brother will have his faults sought out by Allah. And he whose faults are sought by Allah will be exposed by Him (even) in the deepest part of his home."[92]

The hypocrite seeks out a Muslim's faults and he spies on him. Allah says:

> Had they gone forth with you, they would have increased you in nothing but trouble, and would have hurried to and fro in your midst, seeking stir up sedition among you. And among you there are some who would have listened to them. Allah knows well the evildoers. (Qur'an 9:47)

The Prophet (ṣ) said, "If anyone eavesdrops on the conversation of other people while they do not like him to do so or they keep away from him, then lead will be poured into his ears on the Day of Resurrection."[93]

This evil of spying on other Muslims is very common. People must realize that it is the work of the hypocrites. Allah has forbidden us to do it and we must avoid it lest we go on perpetrating a major sin without realizing that our good deeds are wiped out because of it.

---

92 *Al-Tirmidhi*, # 2032.

93 *Al-Bukhari*, # 3916.

CHAPTER 27

To Solicit Praise for What One Has Not Done

Allah warns believers not to seek credit for that which they have not done:

> O you who believe, why do you say that which you do not do? It is most hateful in the sight of Allah to say that which you do not do. (Qur'an 61:2-3)

Abu Sa'id al-Khudri said some hypocrites during the time of the Prophet (ṣ) stayed behind when the Prophet (ṣ) set out for a battle, and they rejoiced at their staying behind. When the Prophet (ṣ) returned, they presented excuses to him and swore (they were telling the truth). They loved to be praised for what they had not done, so these words were revealed:

> "Think not that those who rejoice over what they have carried out and love to be praised for what

> they have not done are safe from chastisement; for them is a painful chastisement" (Qur'an 3:188).

Those who are quick to take credit for what they have not done, or for what other people have done, should heed this.

CHAPTER 28

To Leave a Meeting without Permission

Believers attend meetings to discuss their affairs and the gatherings of Friday and of 'Id. If they are unable to attend, they ask permission to not attend, and if they have to leave the, they ask permission of the host to go. This is what the Companions did. Allah says:

> Those only are believers who believe in Allah and His Messenger and, when they are with him on some common affair, go not away until they ask his leave. Surely those who ask your leave are they who believe in Allah and His Messenger. So if they ask your leave for some affair of theirs, give leave to whom you will of them, and ask Allah's forgiveness for them. Surely Allah is forgiving, merciful. (Qur'an 24:62)

The hypocrites abstained from attending such meetings and from seeking the Prophet's permission.

They slipped out without asking. Allah says:

> Make not the calling of the Messenger among yourselves like your calling one of another. Allah indeed knows those of you who slip away from among you stealthily. So let those who go against His command beware lest a trial befall them, or there befall them a painful chastisement. (Qur'an 24:63)

CHAPTER 29

Reluctance to Take Part in Jihad

Allah says:

> Make ready for them all you can of (armed) force and of horses tethered so that thereby you may dismay the enemy of Allah and your enemy and others beside them whom you know not—Allah knows them. Whatsoever you spend for Allah's cause will be repaid to you in full, and you will not be wronged. (Qur'an 8:60)

The Prophet (ṣ) said, "Practice archery and horse-riding. But that you practice archery is dearer to me than that you ride."[94]

The hypocrite will never make preparations for *jihad*. Allah says:

---

94 *Al-Tirmidhi*, # 1637.

> And if they had intended to go forth, they would certainly have made some preparation for it. But Allah disliked their going forth, so He made them pause, and it was said to them, "Stay back with those who are staying back. (Qur'an 9:46)

The Prophet (ṣ) said, "Whoever dies without having waged *jihad* or having prepared himself in his heart for *jihad* dies as a kind of hypocrite." [95]

Hypocrites do not participate in *jihad* and prevent others from doing so. Allah says:

> Allah indeed knows those among you who hinder (others) and those who say to their brethren, "Come to us." And they come not to the fight but a little. (Qur'an 33:18)

But they cannot avoid death. Allah says:

> Say, "Flight will not do you any good if you fly from death or slaughter, and in that case you will not be allowed to enjoy yourselves but a little." Say, "Who is it that can withhold you from Allah if He intends to do you evil to show you mercy? And they will not find for themselves besides Allah any guardian or a helper. (Qur'an 33:16-17)

---

95 *Muslim*, # 158-1910.

Hypocrites seek excuses to flee from battle. Allah says:

> When a party of them said, "O people of Yathrib, there is no stand for you (here), so go back." And a band of them even sought permission of the Prophet (ṣ), saying, "Our houses are exposed (to the enemy)," though they were not exposed. They desired nothing but to flee. And if an entry had been effected to them from the sides (of the city) and they had been incited to sedition (against the believers), they would certainly have committed it and would have not hesitated about it but slightly. (Qur'an 33:13-14)

Even if hypocrites are in the midst of Muslims, they do not take part in *jihad*. Allah says:

> They think the confederates have not departed, and if the confederates should come (again), they would fain be dwelling among desert Arabs, asking for the news about you. And if they were among you, they would not fight but a little. (Qur'an 33:20)

When the call to *jihad* is heard, hypocrites behave as though they have the pangs of death.

> And those who believe say, "Why has a sūrah not been revealed?" But when a decisive sūrah is

> revealed, and therein fighting is mentioned, you will see those in whose hearts is a disease looking towards you with the look of one who swoons of death. So woe to them. (Qur'an 47:20)

Behaviour in *Jihad*

Hypocrites are afraid of *jihad* and fighting.

> Have you not considered those to whom it was said, "Withhold your hands (from fighting) and establish the prayer and pay *zakah*?" But as soon as fighting is prescribed for them, there is a party of them who fear people as they would fear Allah, or (even) with a greater fear, saying, "Our Lord, why have you prescribed fighting for us? Would you not grant us respite to a near term?" Say, "The comfort of this world is a little trifle and the hereafter is better for him who fears (Allah). And you shall not be wronged a whit." (Qur'an 4:77)

They present false excuses of lacking strength.

> Were it a gain near at hand and a short journey, they would have followed you, but the distance (to Tabuk) was too far for them. Yet they will swear by Allah, "Had we been able, we would certainly have set out with you." They destroy their own souls, and Allah knows that surely they are liars. (Qur'an 9:42)

Allah does not approve that they should be excused without verification.

> Allah forgive you (O Muḥammad)! Why did you permit them (to stay behind), till it had become clear to you which of them spoke the truth and you had known the liars? (Qur'an 9:43)

Only they seek permission to be excused.

> Only those ask leave of you who believe not in Allah and the Last Day and whose hearts are in doubt, so in their doubt they waver. (Qur'an 9:45)

The same applies to wealthy hypocrites.

> And when a sūrah is revealed (saying), "Believe in Allah and strive along with His Messenger," the men of affluence among them ask your permission and say, 'Leave us behind so that we may be with those who stay." (Qur'an 9:86)

So Allah puts a seal on their hearts.

> They are pleased to be with those who stay at home, and a seal has been set on their hearts, so they understand not. (Qur'an 9:87)

> The ground (of complaint) is only against those who ask leave of you while they are rich. They are pleased that they should be with those who stay at home. Allah has set a seal on their hearts, so they

> know not. (Qur'an 9:93)

Even Bedouin hypocrites shy away from *jihad.*

> And there came the excusers from among the desert Arabs, asking for leave; and those who lied to Allah and His Messenger sat at home. Soon a painful chastisement will afflict those of them who disbelieve. (Qur'an 9:90)

On the other hand, Muslims never seek permission to stay away.

> Those who believe in Allah and the Last Day ask no leave of you so that they may (stay away) from struggling hard with their riches and their lives. Allah is knower of the God-fearing. (Qur'an 9:44)

Hypocrites not only stay at home themselves but also hinder other people from taking part in *jihad.*

> Those, who were left behind rejoiced in staying behind the Messenger of Allah, and they abhorred struggling hard with their riches and their lives for the cause of Allah. They said, "Go not forth in the heat." Say, "The fire of Hell is fiercer in heat." Would that they understand (this)! (Qur'an 9:81)

Sometimes, however, they seek to remove from themselves the blot of hypocrisy by asking to be allowed to fight in *jihad.*

> So if Allah brings you back to a party of them, and they ask leave of you to go forth, say, "Never will you go forth with me, nor will you fight any enemy with me. You were pleased to sit back the first time, so now sit back with those who stay behind." (Qur'an 9:83)

Whenever the Prophet (ṣ) returned from *jihad*, the hypocrites who stayed behind gave excuses on oath. Allah instructed the Muslims to leave them alone and not accept their excuses.

> They will excuse themselves to you when you return to them. Say, "Do not excuse yourselves. We shall not believe you; Allah has indeed informed us of your tidings. Allah will certainly see your deed, and so will His Messenger, then you will be brought back to the Knower of the unseen and the seen, then He will inform you of what you used to do." They will soon swear to you by Allah, when you return to them, so that you may leave them alone, so you leave them alone. Surely they are an abomination, and their refuge is Hell, a recompense for that which they used to earn. They swear to you, that you may be pleased with them, yet Allah will never be pleased with the transgressing people. (Qur'an 9:94-96)

Even if hypocrites go to the battlefield, there they

would complain if things were not too pleasing to them. They would have doubts concerning Allah and raise objections to the divine decree.

> Then after sorrow He sent down security on you, a calm coming on a party of you, and (there was) another party whom their own souls had rendered anxious; they entertained about Allah thoughts of ignorance quite unjustly, saying, "We have no hand in the affair." Say, "Surely the affair is wholly (in the hands) of Allah." They conceal in their hearts what they would not reveal to you. They said, "If we had any part in the affair, we would not have been slain here." Say, "Even if you had been in your houses, those for whom slaying was decreed would have gone forth to the place where they lie slaughtered now" so that Allah might test what was in your hearts and so that He might purge what was in your hearts. Allah knows what is in hearts. (Qur'an 3:154)

Abu Talhah said, "On the day of Uhud, drowsiness overtook us while we were in battle rows. My sword dropped down from my hand. I picked it up and it dropped again, and again I picked it up. The other party was that of the hypocrites, who had no concern at all but for themselves, the most cowardly of people, the most frightened, fleeing from the truth.

> 'They thought wrongly of Allah, the thought of ignorance' (Qur'an 3:154).

They lie and doubt Allah's affairs." The hypocrites discouraged the Muslims from going to battle. If any of them was martyred, they would boast that if they had paid heed to their advice, they would have been safe. Allah says:

> O you who believe, be not like the unbelievers, who say of their brethren, when they are travelling through the earth or engaged in fighting, "If they had stayed with us, they would not have died or been slain." This that Allah may make it a cause of sighs and regrets in their hearts. It is Allah that gives life and death, and Allah sees well all that you do. (Qur'an 3:156)

But Allah says to them that they should keep death at bay if they are truthful.

> To those who said of their brethren while they themselves held back, "Had they obeyed us, they would not have been slain," say, "Then avert death from yourselves if you are truthful." (Qur'an 3:168)

Rather, they will face death wherever they go.

> Wheresoever you may be, death will overtake you, though you be in lofty towers. If some good befalls them, they say, "This is from Allah," and if an evil

> befalls them, they say, "This is from you (O Prophet)." Say, "All is from Allah." But what is the matter with these people that they do not understand anything? (Qur'an 4:78)

The hypocrites also pleaded that if a correct *jihad* was being waged, they would have joined definitely. Or, if they had the expertise, they would have fought. Allah says:

> And so that He might determine the hypocrites to whom it was said, "Come, fight for the cause of Allah or defend yourselves." They said, "If we know that fighting is there, we would follow you." On that day they were nearer to disbelief than to belief. They say with their mouths what is not in their hearts. Allah knows best what they conceal. (3:167)

Hypocrites also promise disbelievers that they will help them.

> Have you not considered those who are hypocrites? They say to their brethren who disbelieve from among the people of the Book, "If you are expelled, we will certainly go forth with you and we will never obey anyone against you, and if you are fought against, we will certainly help you." Allah bears witness that they surely are liars. (Qur'an 59:11)

Allah says they are liars and will never fight.

> If they are expelled, never will they go out with them. If they are attacked (in fight), they will never help them. If they do help them, they will turn their backs, so they will receive no help. (Qur'an 59:12)

They present false excuses.

> Those of the desert Arabs who were left behind will soon say to you, "Our possessions and our families kept us occupied, so ask forgiveness for us!" They say with their tongues what is not in their hearts. Say, "Then who can avail you in anything against Allah if He intends to do you harm or He intends to do you good? Nay, Allah is ever aware of what you do." (Qur'an 48:11)

Hypocrites call Muslims stupid because they fight without proper equipment.

> (Recall) when the hypocrites and those in whose hearts was a disease, said, "Their faith has made them crazy," but if anyone puts his trust in Allah, then surely Allah is mighty, wise. (Qur'an 8:49)

Chapter 30
The Conduct of Hypocrites in the Prophet's Time

The hypocrites showed disrespect to the Prophet (ṣ) and called him unjust. Allah says,

> And of them are some who blame you in respect of alms. If they are given something thereof, they are pleased, but if they are not given anything thereof, then they are enraged. (Qur'an 9:58)

Abu Sa'id al-Khudri said about a hypocrite by the name of Dhu al-Khuwaysirah that while the Prophet (ṣ) was distributing some property, a man who belonged to Banu Tamim came and said, "O Messenger of Allah, be fair." He said, "Woe to you! Who will do justice if I do not. If I am not fair, then you will be ruined." 'Umar Ibn al-Khattab said, "Messenger of Allah, permit me to chop his head off."[96]

Allah says,

> And would that they were content with what Allah and His Messenger gave them and would say, "Allah suffices us. Allah will soon give us (more) out of His bounty and His Messenger too. Surely to Allah alone we humbly turn." (Qur'an 9:59)

They also blamed the Prophet (ṣ) for listening to everyone.

> Among them are men who molest the Prophet and say, "He is (all) ear." Say, "He listens to what is best for you. He believes in Allah, has faith in the believers and is a mercy to those of you who believe." But those who molest the Messenger will have a grievous penalty. (Qur'an 9:61)

The hypocrites then denied on oath that they were disrespectful to the Prophet (ṣ).

> They swear by Allah that they said nothing (evil), but indeed they uttered blasphemy, and they did it after accepting Islam; And they meditated a plot which they were unable to carry out. This revenge of theirs was (their) only return for the bounty

96 *Al-Bukhari*, # 3610.

> with which Allah and His Messenger had enriched them! If they repent, it will be best for them, but if they turn back (to their evil ways), Allah will punish them with a grievous penalty in this life and in the hereafter. They will have none on earth to protect or help them. (Qur'an 9:74)

The hypocrites accused 'Aishah of being unfaithful, thereby hurting the Prophet (ṣ) very much.

> Those who brought forward the lie are a body among yourselves. Think it not to be an evil to you. On the contrary, it is good for you. To every man among them (will come the punishment) of the sin that he earned, and to him who took on himself the lead among them will be a penalty grievous. (Qur'an 24:11)

As for the words "him who took on himself the lead among them," she said that they refer to 'Abdullah Ibn Ubayy Ibn Salul.[97]

Imam al-Zuhri said, "I was with Walid Ibn 'Abd al-Malik when he recited the verse 'to him who took on himself the lead among them will be a penalty grievous.' He said that it was revealed concerning 'Ali. But I said to him, 'May Allah correct the emir! It is not

---

97 *Al-Bukhari*, # 4749.

so, as 'Urwah Ibn Zubayr told me on the authority of 'Aishah.' He asked me what he had told me and I said, 'He told me that she said, 'It was revealed concerning 'Abdullah Ibn Ubayy Ibn Salul, the hypocrite.'"[98]

When the Prophet (ṣ) consulted Usamah Ibn Zayd, 'Ali and Barirah, they testified that 'Aishah was chaste and innocent. So he stood up on the pulpit and said, "O you Muslims, who will support me against a man who has hurt me by slandering my family. By Allah, I know of my family nothing but piety. And they have mentioned a man whom I know to be pious. He has never entered my house except with me."[99]

The hypocrites used to create difficulties for the Prophet (ṣ).

> Certainly they sought to stir up sedition before, and have upset matters for you, until the truth arrived, and Allah's command prevailed, though they abhorred it. (Qur'an 9:48)

They conspired against the Prophet (ṣ).

> And they say, "Obedience (is our duty)," but when they go forth from you, a party of them spend the

---

98 *Fath al-Bari*, II.

99 *Al-Bukhari*, # 4750.

> night together in planning other than what you say. And Allah records what they plan by night, so turn away from them and put your trust in Allah. Allah suffices as a guardian. (Qur'an 4:81)

Hypocrites disbelieve the verses and the Prophet (ṣ) and they make fun of him.

> Even as those before you were mightier than you in strength and more affluent than you in wealth and children. They enjoyed their lot awhile, so you enjoy your lot awhile even as those before you did enjoy their lot awhile. And you indulge in idle talk as they indulged. Their deeds are lost in this world and the hereafter, and they are the losers. (Qur'an 9:69)

They attribute their affliction to the Prophet (ṣ)

> Wheresoever you may be, death will overtake you, though you may be in lofty towers." If some good befalls them, they say, "This is from Allah," and if an evil befalls them, they say, "This is from you." Say, "All is from Allah." But what is the matter with these people that they do not understand anything? (Qur'an 4:78)

The hypocrites built a mosque to accommodate evil people and sow dissension among the Muslims.

> Those who have set up a mosque to hurl and to promote disbelief, to cause division among the believers and to make it a place of ambush for one who has made war against Allah and His Messenger aforetime, they will certainly swear, "We desired nothing but good." Allah bears witness that they are certainly liars. (Qur'an 9:107)

> You should never stand therein. Surely a mosque founded from the first day on piety is worthier that you should stand therein. In it are men who love to purify themselves, and Allah loves those who purify themselves. (Qur'an 9:108)

They would vanish when the Qur'an was revealed concerning their misdeeds.

> And whenever a sūrah is revealed, they look at one another (saying), "Does anyone see you?" Then they turn away. Allah has turned away their hearts because they are a people who understand not. (Qur'an 9:127)

Hypocrites are afraid of being exposed.

> The hypocrites fear lest a sūrah should be sent down about them, informing them of what is in their hearts. Say, "Go on mocking; surely Allah will bring forth what you fear. (Qur'an 9:64)

They would go to the infidels for a judgement. But

if it was unfavourable to them, then they rushed to the Prophet (ṣ) for a redress. They would plead that their aim was pious.

> But how will it be when misfortune befalls them on account of what their hands have sent before? Then they will come to you swearing by Allah, "We did not desire (anything) but good and concord." (Qur'an 4:62)

> Those are the ones the secrets of whose hearts Allah knows. So turn away from them, admonish them and speak to them a word appealing to their souls. (Qur'an 4:63)

The hypocrites retreated even before fighting began in the battle of Uhud.

When the Prophet (ṣ) offered the *fajr* prayer at Shawt and the enemy were so near that they could see one another, 'Abdullah Ibn Ubayy, the hypocrite, put forward an excuse. He took away one-third of the army with him, saying that he could not understand why they should play with their lives. He was unhappy that the Prophet (ṣ) had preferred the advice of someone else to that of his own. Zayd Ibn Thabit said that, after that, the Companions were divided into two parties: one that pledged to fight against the deserters, and another that disagreed with them and said that they would not fight against them. So these words were revealed:

> What is the matter with you that there are two parties (among you) concerning the hypocrites while Allah has made them to retract (to disbelief) because of what they have earned? (Qur'an 4:88)

He said further that the Prophet (ṣ) said, "That ... removes sins just as fire removes impurities from silver."[100]

Hypocrites lend no ear

> And be not like those who say "We have heard" while they hear not. (Qur'an 8:21)

They attend the gatherings of infidels

> And He has indeed revealed to you in the Book that when you hear the revelations of Allah being disbelieved and mocked at, sit not with them (who do this) until they indulge in a discourse other than that, or else you would indeed be like them. Surely Allah will gather together the hypocrites and the disbelievers in Hell. (Qur'an 4:140)

---

100 *Al-Bukhari*, # 4050.

> You will see those in whose hearts is a disease hastening towards them, saying, "We fear lest a turn of fortune should befall us." But it may be that Allah will soon bring the victory or a commandment from Himself, then they will become remorseful over what they conceal in their souls. (Qur'an 5:52)

Hypocrites spread rumours

> And when there comes to them any tiding, whether of peace or of fear, they spread it abroad. If they had only referred it to the Messenger and to those in authority from among them, then those among them who can search the truth about it would have known the matter. And were it not for the bounty of Allah to you and His mercy, you would have followed Satan, except a few. (Qur'an 4:83)

There are people who are quick to pass on news without giving a thought to the consequences. The result is that many people get disheartened and turn away from religion. Hence, such people must first consult the responsible individuals.

Chapter 31

Allah's Promise to Hypocrites

Allah promises hypocrites Hell.

> Allah has promised hypocrites, male and female, and disbelievers the fire of Hell, in which they will abide; That will suffice them. Allah has cursed them, and for them will be a lasting chastisement. (Qur'an 9:68)
>
> Allah has prepared for them a severe chastisement. Surely vile is what they have been doing. (Qur'an 58: 15)
>
> Neither their richness nor their children will avail them in anything against Allah. They are companions of the Fire. They will abide therein. (Qur'an 58:17)
>
> So let not their riches nor their children elate you. Allah intends only to chastise them in the life of this world and that their souls should depart while

they are disbelievers. (Qur'an 9:55)

Do they not see that they are tried every year once or twice? Yet they repent not, nor are they admonished. (Qur'an 9:126)

But as for those in whose hearts is a disease, it only adds abomination to their abomination, and they die while they are disbelievers. (Qur'an 9:125)

You ask forgiveness for them or you ask not forgiveness for them. Even if you ask forgiveness for them seventy times, Allah will not forgive them. This is because they disbelieved in Allah and His Messenger. Allah guides not the transgressing people. (Qur'an 9:80)

And never pray over any one of them that may die, nor stand over his grave. Surely they disbelieved in Allah and His Messenger, and they died while they were transgressors. (Qur'an 9:84)

Accursed they will remain. Wherever they are found, they will be seized and slain relentlessly. (Qur'an 33:61)

If We will, We would show them to you, then you would know them by their marks. And certainly you can recognize them by the tone of (their) speech. Allah knows your deeds. (Qur'an 47:30)

And among those around you of the desert Arabs

> there are some hypocrites, and among the people of Madinah there are some who persist in hypocrisy. You know them not; We know them. We shall chastise them twice, then they will be turned back to a mighty chastisement. (Qur'an 9:101)

Ibn 'Abbas said that Allah's Messenger stood up to deliver the Friday sermon and said, "O so-and-so, get out, for you are a hypocrite. O you, get out; you too are a hypocrite." So he expelled them by their names, disgracing them. 'Umar was not there for the Friday prayer that day because of something that kept him away. He met them while they were leaving the mosque. He kept himself away from them, ashamed that he had not come. He thought that the people had dispersed, while they too hid themselves from 'Umar, imagining that he knew of their case. 'Umar entered the mosque and found that the people had not yet offered the prayer. A Muslim man said to him, "Be happy, O 'Umar! Allah has disgraced the hypocrites. This is the first punishment the—Prophet's making them leave the mosque—and the second punishment is chastisement in the grave."[101]

---

101 *Sifah al-Nifaq*, # 178; *Tafsir Ibn Kathir*, 2/423.

Allah did not accept any pious deed of the hypocrites. Mu'awiyah al-Hudhali said, "The hypocrite offers the prayer but Allah rejects it. He fasts but Allah rejects it. He gives charity but Allah rejects it. He fights in battle but Allah rejects it. And he is slain and Allah puts him in Hell."

Though he may participate in *jihad* and attain martyrdom, that does not wipe out his hypocrisy.

The Prophet (ṣ) said, "There are three kinds of martyrs. A believing man takes part in *jihad* with his life and his property for Allah's cause till he meets the enemy and fights until he is killed. This martyr is worthy of pride. He will be in the tent of Allah under His throne. Even a prophet does not surpass him for any reason except the excellence and superiority of the rank of prophethood. A second believing man who has wronged himself with sins and lapses exceeds in *jihad* with his life and property for Allah's cause till he meets the enemy and fights against them till he is killed. He is forgiven his sins and lapses because the sword erases the sins. He will be admitted into paradise from any of the gates of paradise, which has eight gates, while Hell has seven gates, some of paradise being more excellent than others. The third martyr is a hypocrite who wages *jihad* with his life and his property for Allah's cause till he meets the enemy and engages them till he is slain. But he goes to Hell. Surely, the sword does not erase hypocrisy."

How the Prophet (ṣ) was expected to treat the Hypocrites

> O Prophet, fear Allah, and obey not the disbelievers and the hypocrites. Surely Allah is ever knowing, wise. (Qur'an 33:1)
>
> O Prophet, carry out *jihad* against the disbelievers and the hypocrites, and be harsh with them. Their refuge is Hell. It is an evil destination. (Qur'an 9:73)
>
> Say, "Expend willingly or unwillingly; it will not be accepted from you, for you are surely a transgressing people. (Qur'an 9:53)
>
> Nothing prevents their spending from being accepted from them except that they disbelieve in Allah and His Messenger, that they come not to offer the prayer but sluggishly and that they expend not but unwillingly. (Qur'an 9:54)

'Umar said, "When 'Abdullah Ibn Ubayy Ibn Salul died, the Prophet was invited to offer the prayer for him. When he stood (before the body), I jumped over towards him and said, 'O Messenger of Allah, will you offer the (funeral) prayer for Ibn Ubayy despite the fact that he had said such-and-such on such-and-such a day?' I began mentioning all the things he had said. Then he smiled and said 'Move back, O 'Umar.' When I became insistent, he said, 'I have been given a choice, so I have chosen. And if I knew that he would be forgiven if I asked Allah's forgiveness more than seventy times, then indeed I would do so.' Then he offered the prayer and moved aside. He had not been aside long when this verse was revealed:

> Never offer prayer for any one of them who dies and do not stand by his grave; surely they disbelieve in Allah and His Messenger and they shall die in transgression. (Qur'an 9:84)

After that, the Prophet never offered the prayer for any hypocrite or stood at the grave of anyone of them till his death."[102]

---

102 *Al-Bukhari*, # 1366.

CHAPTER 32
Some Examples of Hypocrites

First Example

> Their parable is like the parable of one who kindled a fire, but when it had illumined all around him, Allah took away their light and left them in utter darkness—they do not see. Deaf, dumb (and) blind, so they will not turn back. (Qur'an 2:17-18)

Ibn Mas'ud said that when the Prophet (ṣ) came to Madinah, some people who had become Muslim turned hypocrites. They were like someone in darkness who lit a light and could see everything around him, but when the light extinguished suddenly, he could not say what was harmful around him. The hypocrite was a disbeliever when he saw the light of Islam and realized what was lawful and unlawful, good and evil. But he returns to hypocrisy and thus loses the distinction between the lawful and unlawful, good and evil.[103]

Second Example

> Or like abundant rain from the cloud in which is utter darkness and thunder and lightning; they put their fingers into their ears because of the thunder peal, for fear of death, and Allah encompasses the unbelievers. The lightning almost takes away their sight. Whenever it shines on them, they walk in it, and when it becomes dark to them, they stand still. If Allah had pleased, He would certainly have taken away their hearing and their sight; surely Allah has power over all things. (Qur'an 2:19-20)

> This kind of hypocrite sees the truth sometimes and has doubts at other times. His doubts are like the rain in the darkness. Allah also says "they think every shout is against them" (Qur'an 63:4).

> And they swear by Allah that they are most surely of you, and they are not of you, but they are a people who are afraid (of you). If they could find a refuge or cave or a place to enter, they would certainly have turned thereto, running away in all haste. (Qur'an 9:56-57)

---

103 *Tafsir Ibn Kathir.*

When the light of Islam falls on them, some of it enters their hearts. They join Muslims, but when Islam faces some difficulty, they leave them.

Third Example

The Prophet (ṣ) said, "The believer is like a fresh, soft plant, which the wind bends sometimes and straightens sometimes. The hypocrite is like a pine tree, which will not cease to remain straight till it is suddenly uprooted one day."[104]

Allah involves a Muslim in various difficulties and sicknesses so that his sins are washed away. The Prophet (ṣ) said, "No Muslim is afflicted by hardship, fatigue, worry, grief and the like, even by the pricking of a thorn, without Allah making it an expiation for his sins."[105]

As for a hypocrite, it makes no difference whether he suffers an illness or faces a difficulty. His illness is sudden and final. Therefore, he is compared to the pine tree.

---

104 *Al-Bukhari*, # 5643.

105 *Al-Bukhari*, # 5641.

Fourth Example

The Prophet (ṣ) compared the believer who recites the Qur'an and abides by its teachings to a citron, which has a sweet taste and smell. The believer who does not recite the Qur'an but abides by it is like a date, which tastes sweet but has no fragrance. The hypocrite who recites the Qur'an is like a basil, which has a sweet smell but bitter taste. The hypocrite who does not recite the Qur'an is like a colocynth, which has a bitter taste and no smell.[106]

The inward and outward of a believer are the same. Whatever he says with his tongue, he is convinced of in his heart. But a hypocrite is excellent outwardly, though his inward is quite the opposite.

Fifth Example

The hypocrite is restless. He moves here and there in search of peace. He is neither with the Muslims nor with the infidels. Allah says:

> Wavering between that (and this), belonging neither to these nor to those. If Allah sends

106 *Al-Bukhari*, # 5427.

someone astray, you will not find a way for him. (Qur'an 4:143)

The Prophet (ṣ) said, "A hypocrite is like an ewe that moves from one flock to another, not knowing which one to follow."[107]

107 *Muslim*, # 17.

CHAPTER 33

The Hypocrite's Fate after Death

In the Grave

After the hypocrite is buried, his fate is no different than a disbeliever's. The Prophet (ṣ) said, "He will meet the third and say to him the same words (as before), and he will respond, 'My Lord, I believed in you, your Book and your messengers. I offered the prayer, I fasted and I gave the *zakah*,' and he will mention as many good things as he can. Allah will say, 'Stop here.' Then it will be said to him, 'Now we bring to you our witnesses.' He will wonder to himself who could testify against him. So his mouth will be sealed and it will be said to his thighs, his flesh and his bones, 'Speak!' And they will speak concerning his deeds. This will be in order that justice might be dispensed to him and Allah will be angry with that hypocrite."[108]

In the Hereafter

When hypocrites are revived on the Day of Resurrection, they will swear and affirm, "We are Muslims, we lived among Muslims and we have proof of that." Allah says:

> On the day when Allah will raise them up all together, they will swear to Him as they swear to you, and they think that they have something. Behold, surely they are the liars! (Qur'an 58:18)

> On the day when hypocrites, male and female, will say to those who believed, "Wait for us so that we may borrow from your light!" It will be said, "Turn back and seek a light!" Then a wall will be set up between them, having a door, inside which is mercy and outside which is chastisement. They will cry out to them, "Were we not with you?" They will say, "Yea, but you tempted your souls, and you waited, and you doubted, and (your) vain desires beguiled you, until Allah's commandment came and the arch beguiler beguiled you concerning Allah. So this day no ransom will be taken from

108 *Muslim*, #16-2968.

> you, nor from those who disbelieved. Your abode is the Fire. That is your patron and it is an evil destination." (57:13-15)
>
> Surely Allah will gather together the hypocrites and the disbelievers all in Hell. (Qur'an 4:140)
>
> Give the hypocrites tidings of a painful chastisement for them. (Qur'an 4:138)
>
> Surely the hypocrites will be in the lowest depth of the Fire, and you will not find for them any helper. (Qur'an 4:145)

Allah will not conceal the faults of the hypocrites, but will conceal those of the believers. The Prophet (ṣ) said,

> "Allah Most High will draw the believer nearer to Him and put over him His veil and conceal him from people and recall his sins. He will ask, 'Do you remember that sin?' He will say, "Yes, my Lord," and He will recall them all, so that he will imagine to himself that he is ruined. He (Allah) will say, 'I concealed them for you in the world and today I forgive them for you.' Then he will be given his book of accounts in his right hand. But as for the disbeliever and the hypocrite, they will be called in the presence of the (entire) creation. 'These are they who lied against their Lord. Behold! The curse of Allah will be on the evildoers'

(Qur'an 11:18)."[109]

The hypocrite will be the worst of men on the Day of Resurrection. Allah's Messenger (ṣ) said, "Surely the most evil of people is the two-faced one. He comes to these with a face and to those with another face."[110]

---

109 *Al-Bukhari*, # 2441, 4685.

110 *Al-Bukhari*, # 3494.

Chapter 34
Hypocrisy a Disease To Be Always Feared

Hypocrisy is a disease that drives faith out of a person's heart. Sometimes, a person is unaware that hypocrisy has made a home in his heart and he performs the deeds of a hypocrite unknowingly.

'Abdullah Ibn Mas'ud said, "A man among you goes out and meets someone with whom he did some work. He speaks to him of this and that and praises him highly. He is most likely not to get his task done, yet he returns having made Allah angry and not possessing anything of religion."[111]

Here are some words from the Companions showing how fearful they were of hypocrisy.

---

111 Al-Faryabi, *Sifah al- Nifaq*, # 111.

Abu Ayyub al-Ansari said, "There will be times when a person does not have a needle's worth of hypocrisy in him. But there will also be times when he does not have a needle's worth of faith in him."[112]

Jubayr Ibn Nufayr said that he heard Abu al-Darda' while he was finishing his prayer. He sought refuge in Allah from hypocrisy again and again. Jubayr asked him, "What's with you, O Abu al-Darda'? ... He said, "Leave me alone. By Allah, a man turns away from his religion in just a moment and leaves it."[113]

Aban asked al-Hasan, "What gives me security from hypocrisy when (even) 'Umar Ibn al-Khattab was fearful of it?"[114] He also said that when they saw hypocrisy devouring faith, they had no grief other than about hypocrisy.[115]

Al-Mu'alla Ibn Ziyad said that he had heard al-Hasan say, "By Allah, besides whom there is no god,

---

112 Ibid., # 77.

113 Ibid., # 73.

114 Ibid.

115 Ibid., # 82.

there has never been, nor will there ever be, a believer who has no fear of hypocrisy. And there has never been, nor will there ever be, a hypocrite who fears hypocrisy. He who does not fear hypocrisy is a hypocrite."[116]

> Muḥammad Ibn Sirin said that nothing is more frightening than hypocrisy to someone who has read this verse: "And of mankind there are some who say, 'We believe in Allah and the Last Day,' while they are not believers" (Qur'an 2:8).[117]

'Amr Ibn al-Aswad al-Ansi would hold his left hand with his right when he went to the mosque. When asked about this, he said, "I fear lest my hands become hypocrites."[118]

Salam Ibn Abi Muti' that Ayyub had with him a man of the Murji'ah, who said that there is either disbelief or faith (no third). Ayyub did not say anything (for sometime) and then turned to him and asked him if he had read Allah's words,

"And others who await Allah's commandment,

---

116 Ibid., # 87.

117 Ibid., # 89.

118 Ibid., # 90.

> whether He chastises them or relents towards them" (Qur'an 9:106)

and whether they are believers or disbelievers. The man was nonplussed. Ayyub said, "Go and recite the Qur'an. Each verse mentions hypocrisy. And I fear for myself."[119]

'Umar, the slave of Ghufrah, said, "The furthest of men from hypocrisy and the most fearful of them for himself is the one who finds that nothing can save him from it. And the nearest of men to it is the one who gets peace of mind from being praised for something he does not possess. When you are praised for something you do not possess, say, 'O Allah forgive me for that which they do not know and do not take me to account for what they say. Surely, you know while they do not."[120]

Ibrahim al-Taymi said, "When I compare my words with my deeds, I fear lest I be a denier (of the Shari'ah)."[121]

---

119 Ibid., # 92.

120 Ibid., # 94.

121 Ibid., # 95.

Ibn Abi Mulaykah said, "I met thirty of the Prophet's Companions and each one of them feared hypocrisy. There was none among them who said that he had the faith of Jibril or Mika'il."[122]

---

122 *Al-Bukhari.*

CHAPTER 35

Hypocrisy Will Be More Common before the Last Days

'Aishah said that when Allah's Messenger (ṣ) died, hypocrisy was visible in Madinah and the Arabs apostatized.[123]

Hudhayfah said, "If a man among you spoke in the time of the Prophet (ṣ), he became a hypocrite because of it. But, today, I hear it from one of you ten times."[124]

Allah's Messenger (ṣ) said, "What I fear most for my *ummah* is every glib-tongued hypocrite."[125]

---

123 Al-Asbahani, *Sifah al-Nifaq*, # 117.

124 *Ahmad*, # 23191.

125 *Al-Jami' al-Saghir*, # 239.

Al-Hasan said, "Ahnaf Ibn Qays came to 'Umar in a deputation. 'Umar held him for a year and then asked him if he knew why he had restrained him. Then he said, 'Surely, Allah's Messenger cautioned us against every hypocrite, master of the tongue. You are not one of them, if Allah wills; so go to your native land.'"[126]

'Umar Ibn al-Khattab said, "Three things destroy Islam: the straying of a scholar, the hypocrite's debating with the Qur'an and the misleading imams (who rule and lead)."[127]

Hudhayfah said, "The hypocrites who are among you today are worse than the hypocrites in the time of Allah's Messenger (ṣ)." Someone asked him, "O Abu 'Abdullah, how is that?" He said, "Those people used to conceal their hypocrisy, while these make it known."[128]

Allah's Messenger (ṣ) said, "Before the Last Hour, there will be *fitnah* (trials and mischief) like pieces of a dark night. A man will arise in the morning as a

---

126 Al-Asbahani, *Sifah al-Nifaq*, # 148.

127 Al-Faryabi, *Sifah al-Nifaq*, # 31.

128 Ibid., # 53.

believer but the evening will find him to be a disbeliever. And people will sell their religion for worldly possessions."[129]

'Abdullah Ibn 'Umar said, "A time will come when people will assemble in their mosques but there will not be among them a believer."[130]

129 *Al-Tirmidhi*, # 2197.

130 Al-Faryabi, *Sifah al-Nifaq*, # 108.

CHAPTER 36

Treatment of Hypocrites in Current Times

They must not be obeyed.

> O Prophet, fear God and obey not the disbelievers and hypocrites. Lo! Allah is all-knowing, wise. (Qur'an 33:1).

> You are those who love them, but they love you not, even though you believe in all the (revealed) Books. When they meet you, they say, "We believe," and when they are alone, they bite their fingertips at you in rage. Say, "Perish in your rage. Surly Allah knows what is in hearts." (Qur'an 3:119)

Hypocrites must not be made happy, as we learn from 'Umar Ibn 'Abd al-'Aziz. Abu Qalabah was taken ill in the Levant, so 'Umar Ibn 'Abd al-'Aziz visited him and said, "O Abu Qalabah ... let not hypocrites be happy because of us."[131]

The funeral prayer should not be offered for them. The Prophet (ṣ) was also forbidden to do so, as we learned in the previous chapter.

---

131 Al-Faryabi, *Sifah al- Nifaq*, # 60.

CHAPTER 37

The Straying of Muslims in the Last Days

Yazid Ibn ʿAmirah said that whenever Muʿadh Ibn Jabal sat down to preach, he would say while sitting, "Allah is a just ruler. His name is blessed. Those who doubt will perish." One day, Muʿadh Ibn Jabal said, "Surely, ahead of you are trials in which there will be abundant wealth and the Qur'an will be so easy that everyone will learn it, the believer and the hypocrite, man and woman, the young and the old, the free man and the slave. Soon a man will say, 'Why do the people not follow me, though I have recited the Qur'an? They will not follow me till I introduce for them something other than it.' Hence, beware of innovations! Surely, that which is innovated is error (and misleading). And I warn you against the straying of the wise (scholar), for the Devil utters a word of error from the tongue of the scholar, while the hypocrite may utter a true word sometimes."[132]

Al-Hasan said, "The Last Hour will not come till every people are governed by their hypocrites."[133]

---

132 *Abu Dawud*, # 4611.

133 Al-Faryabi, *Sifah al-Nifaq*, # 117.

Index